HO'
JUDAISM
TO YOUR
NON-JEWISH
NEIGHBOR

HOW TO EXPLAIN JUDAISM TO YOUR NON-JEWISH NEIGHBOR

By Rabbi Edward Zerin, Ph.D.

Isaac Nathan Publishing Co., Inc.

Los Angeles

1997

First Edition

Library of Congress Cataloging-in-Publication Data

Edward Zerin, Ph.D.

How to Explain Judaism to Your non-Jewish Neighbors

1. Judaism   2. Jewish Practices

3. Judaism & Christianity   4. Christianity & Judaism

ISBN 0-914615-20-3

Library of Congress Catalog Card Number: 96-69660

Manufactured in the United States of America

Isaac Nathan Publishing Co., Inc.
22711 Cass Avenue
Woodland Hills, California, 91364
(818) 225-9631

In Judaism there is no dogma, no fixed creed, with
which a Jewish person must agree completely.

The test of loyalty in Judaism is how one acts
and not how one thinks.

Our Rabbis taught :

The righteous of all people have a share in the world to come.

(Tosefta Sanhedrin 13.2)

"When your children ask you, 'What do you mean by this
rite?' you shall tell them . . ."

(Exodus 12:26-27)

When Jews say either "Hello" or "Good-bye,"
we often use the Hebrew word—*Shalom.*

Shalom means *peace.*

Foreward - 1954

The freedom of worship we enjoy in America is a distinctive feature of our democracy, We are free to be different.

This freedom finds natural expression in our religious diversity. Today in our nation, there are approximately sixty million Protestants, thirty-six million Roman Catholics, two-and-a half Greek Orthodox Catholics, and five-and-one-half million Jews.*

The presence of so many religious groups could produce tension and conflict. However, we can maintain relaxed, permissive relationships when we learn to understand, accept, and respect each other, This volume should give us new understanding and appreciation of one major religious group.

Rabbi Edward Zerin gives us more than casual reading. Historical background and contemporary orientation are presented in orderly development. He reveals both the mood and mode of Judaism, which will make every reader a better neighbor and citizen—possibly a better member of their faith.

Dr. Zerin opens the door to Judaism and invites us in.

Lloyd H. Olson
Iowa and Quad-Cities Regional Director
The National Conference of Christians and Jews
1954

* This INTRODUCTION appeared in the 1954 version of the present book which was published by Abingdon Press under the title *Our Jewish Neighbors,* The affiliation figures with each religion are those of 1954. Judaism has remained the same at five-and-a-half million. However, the message retains its original validity and speaks with equal cogence to the America about to enter the twenty-first century.

Foreward - 1997

On April 13, 1986, Pope John Paul II became the first bishop of Rome to visit the Great synagogue of that ancient city since St. Peter, who as a Jew doubtlessly himself prayed often in an earlier version of Rome's central synagogue, As the Pope and the Chief Rabbi crossed the threshold to enter the Synagogue, the Jewish chorus inside, which had been singing a psalm, joyously cried out, "Halleluia!" or as my fellow Christians and I would say, "Praise the Lord!" It was a significant moment in the two millennia long, too often tragic history of Jews and Christians. But it was also, in the root sense of the term, "typical" of our age, a defining moment that tells us much about what is best about our time.

Such spiritual exchanges of the riches of our ancient religious heritages are thankfully no longer rare between Christian leaders, whether Protestant or Orthodox or Catholic, and Jewish leaders. They mark new hope for the future as we enter the third millennium of Jewish-Christian relations. This book provides an insightful introduction to Judaism for Christians, Reading it, then, is more than an exercise in good neighborliness. It provides Christians with the opportunity to be introduced to a world of spiritual wealth from God's People, the Jews, a religious tradition from which we Christians cannot afford to be cut off. Together in response to the call of the One God, we Jews and Christians can not only learn to give to each other what we have learned from our own centuries-long contemplations of the Sacred Scriptures, we can also learn how to share those treasures with others in a way that can help to "mend the world" (*tikkun olam*) as it is said in Jewish tradition.

Dr. Eugene J. Fisher
National Conference of Catholic Bishops
Secretariat for Ecumenical and Interreligious Affairs
January 1997

Foreward - 1997

Twenty-five years ago most Christians in America had never met a Jew in person. Now, many Americans have someone who is Jewish as a member of their family through inter-marriage.

The questions Christians ask about Jewish beliefs and practices may sound elementary, but to the questioner the answer often fills a gaping void.

Rabbi Zerin, in this book, supplies a great many of the answers and, in addition, raises other issues that Christians should be asking when contemplating the faith and the background of a Jew.

In clear and concise terms, this book is an excellent primer for those who want an adult understanding of Jews and Judaism.

Rabbi Isaiah Zeldin
Stephen S. Wise Temple
Los Angeles California
February 1996

Preface

Our rabbis have taught very clearly that being Jewish does not guarantee one's being rewarded either in this life or in life after death. According to them, the test for all people, Jewish and non-Jewish alike, is not what they believe but how they live with themselves and with other people. They said righteousness and lovingkindness (justice and compassion) are the primary requirements for everybody, and those who wish to become Jewish can do so by voluntarily taking on the extra teachings and practices of Judaism.

All interpretations of Judaism hold that salvation can be found through many faiths, if those religions teach their followers to live together with people of all religions in righteousness and loving-kindness.

Whenever you read something that jars you or about which you have a question, I invite you to contact your rabbi or a person learned in Jewish life. You may want to take out a library book or purchase a book that offers a more detailed account of Judaism and the Jewish People.

For some of you this study will be a welcome review; for others it will be like an appetizer, a foretaste of a much larger feast. Wherever you are in your life, my wish is that you will enter upon this journey as an adventurous exploration of a 4,000 year old tradition that continues to grow and strives to meet the challenges of a changing world.

Rabbi Edward Zerin, Ph.D.
Westlake Village, California

Acknowledgements

This book could not have been written without the support of friends and professionals who, like the author, believe in its merit, There are three whose efforts were of immeasurable assistance. JoAnn Haag, drawing upon her rich religious background, indicated subtle points of significance to highlight the message for Christian readers. Dolly Edmonds, retiring after more than forty years with major publishers, brought greater clarity and structure to the work. To my publisher and indefatigable editor, David W. Epstein, I owe a great debt of gratitude. For him, as for me, this publication has been a labor of love.

I want to thank Rabbis Stephen Einstein, Harry Essrig and Eugene Labovitz for their reading and comments on the current manuscript from the various points of view of different denominations within Judaism.

There is one more person whom I want to acknowledge. My wife of fifty years, Marjory, read the manuscript with her usual loving care and critical skill. To her I am grateful for the many enrichments to this book.

This present volume, moreover is indebted to the many men and women of all ages, whether students, teachers, seekers of knowledge or devoted members of the various religious faiths who over the years have shared with me their interest in Judaism.

Rabbi Edward Zerin
Westlake Village, CA
February 1997

CONTENTS

Glossaries & Lists

This proposed seal for the United States was submitted for consideration by the committee of Jefferson, Franklin and Adams in August, 1776. It depicts the Israelites having crossed the Red Sea and the destruction of the Pharoah's army.

American Heritage Haggadah, Gefen Publishing, Jerusalem, 1992

Chapter One
The Jewish People
Come to the United States

JEWISH LIFE IN THE UNITED STATES IS OVER 300 YEARS OLD. Some people say it is even older. It is reported that the first person to come ashore when Columbus discovered America was his interpreter, Luis de Torres, who had been born of Jewish parents.

Thirty-four years after the Pilgrims landed at Plymouth Rock in 1620, a group of twenty-one Jews landed in the port of New York, then called New Amsterdam. The year was 1654. This landing was the beginning of the first permanent settlement of Jewish People in the United States.

From this small beginning, Jewish life in the United States grew. At the time of the American Revolution, nearly 2,000 Jewish People lived in the Colonies. Many Jews served with George Washington in the battles of the Revolutionary War. In fact, George Washington often turned to his Jewish friend Haym Salomon when he needed help.

When the Colonial troops were encamped, hungry and barefooted at Valley Forge, Washington sent an urgent message to Haym Salomon. The messenger arrived while Salomon and his fellow Jews were in synagogue. It was *Yom Kippur—the Day of Atonement*—the most important religious day of the Jewish

Calendar Year Identification
B.C.E. & C.E. versus B.C. & A.D.

Christianity uses the Julian Calendar where years are counted from the birth of Jesus.

Judaism uses both the Jewish Calendar for religious purposes which begins with the biblical dating of Creation, and Julian Calendar as the dating of the common culture.

Christian dating is based on the approximate birth of Jesus.

B.C. = Before Christ

A.D. = After Christ

(*Ano Domini*—"in the year of our Lord.")

Jewish dating using the Julian Calendar uses different suffixes for the same dates:

B.C.E. = Before the Common Era

C.E. = Common Era

Both are identical.

Jewish terminology deletes the use of the name of Jesus.

For an explanation of the Jewish Calendar see page 35.

year. When Salomon heard of the desperate situation of the American troops, he asked that the services be interrupted. He described the plight of General Washington and his troops to the members of the congregation, who immediately promised the necessary funds. Washington and the army received the needed aid, and they marched on to victory.

As the United States pushed its frontiers forward, many Jews moved westward with the other pioneers. Jews reached the Mississippi River, which they crossed in their covered wagons. They settled in the prairie states. They wandered to Texas, fought and died with Davy Crockett at the Alamo. They climbed the Rocky Mountains and explored the far West.

Of the more than five million American citizens who identify themselves as Jews—some do so in terms of our religion, others because of our ethnic and/or cultural heritage, and some because of being born of a Jewish mother or father. Many others are *Jews by Choice*, having converted to Judaism. Jews live in the big cities and in the small towns. Some of us are professional people; others farm the land or work in factories. A great many have established their own businesses.

We came to the United States from many countries of the world. At first we came from the lands of the once great Spanish Empire. Later, we arrived from Central Europe, particularly Germany. Most of the Jewish young people whom you meet today were born in the United States. Many of their parents and grandparents, however, came to this country to escape the cruel prejudice of Russia, Poland, Rumania, and other countries of Eastern Europe. The last three large immigrations consisted mostly of survivors of the Holocaust, Jews fleeing Iran after the fall of the Shah and, most recently, Jews released from Russia.

Following the French Revolution and the emancipation of the Jewish People from the Medieval ghettos, the four groups of contemporary Judaism took form. The first was Reform Judaism, followed in turn by Modern Orthodoxy, Conservative Judaism, and, in the 20th Century, Reconstructionist Judaism.

Judaism emphasizes three themes: **God, Torah** and **Israel.** **God** represents the Source of Revelation, the Creator of the World and Master of the Universe. **Torah** has two meanings. Torah refers to the *Five Books of Moses—Genesis, Exodus, Leviticus, Numbers* and *Deuteronomy*. Torah also refers to the vast tradition of Jewish law and culture based upon the Five *Books of Moses*. The term **Israel** refers to the Jewish People and its relationship to the peoples of the world.

Orthodox Jews

Orthodox Jews observe the Jewish tradition in the same manner in which our ancestors did for many years. They call their house of worship a synagogue or a *shul*, since they believe that only the Holy Temple in ancient Jerusalem should be called a *temple*. In their worship they pray in Hebrew. Men and women are seated separately, and the men worship with their heads covered. Orthodox Jews observe what Jews call the dietary laws.

Jews who follow these dietary laws will not eat pork; they eat the meat only of those animals which have cloven (split) hooves and chew their cud. Animals must be slaughtered in special ways so that the animal suffers little, if at all.

Orthodox Jews will eat only seafood that has both fins and scales, as set forth in the *Torah*. They keep separate sets of dishes for meat and dairy foods, and use separate soap and dish towels as well as storage space for each. Orthodox Jews will wait a procribed period of time before eating dairy foods following a meat meal. All this is called keeping *kosher*.

Orthodox Jews also believe that the *Torah*—the first five books in the Bible called the *Five Books of Moses*—was revealed to Moses at Mt. Sinai by God, and that there are 613 commandments or laws found in the *Torah* which represent a perfect and permanent set of commandments. They also believe that God revealed at Sinai the proper procedures for interpreting these laws in future situations.

Reform Jews

Reform Jews have changed many of the traditional Jewish ways and dropped others. They hold that some forms of religion should change as life itself changes. Their house of worship usually is called a temple. In worshipping, their prayers are recited both in Hebrew and in English, and men and women tend to sit together in family groups. While men are neither required to cover their heads nor to observe the dietary laws, many Reform Jews do worship with their heads covered and also observe some aspects of the *kosher* tradition. In contrast to Orthodox Jews, however, they believe that the *Five Books of Moses* are of human authorship, though inspired by God. While the *Torah* remains as a guide, Reform Jews believe that God's purpose is being understood anew and reinterpreted with each generation.

Conservative Jews

The third group consists of Conservative Jews. Sometimes the Conservative congregation leans closer to the Orthodox way,

Jewish Population Figures

How many Jewish people do you think there are in the world today? Take a guess.

Some people answer, "50,000,000."

Others say, "100,000,000."

Still others say, "200,000,000!"

The correct answer as of 1993 is only 12,963,000 Jews in a world of almost six billion people.*

The largest single group of Jews lives in the United States. 5,650,000 of the approximately 270,000,000 Americans are Jewish.

Jews also live in all of the five continents of the world.

Europe (Including Eastern and Western Europe and the Balkans)	1,872,700
Americas (North, South and Central)	6,440,500
Asia (Including Israel)	4,444,400
Africa	109,800
Australia & New Zealand	95,600
Total	**12,963,000**

This book is about the 5,650,000 Jews who live in the United States.

* Statistics for 1993 from the *American Jewish Year Book-1995,* Vol. 95, American Jewish Committee, NY.

and at other times it may resemble the Reform group. Conservative Judaism upholds the dietary laws but uses both Hebrew and English in their prayer services. In most Conservative congregations men and women sit together, while in some, women sit in a separate section. Conservative Jewish men always pray with their heads covered.

Conservative Jews vary in their beliefs about the origin of the *Torah*. The more traditional members believe in Divine authorship, while the more liberal incline toward human origin. However, in interpreting Jewish laws and customs, Conservative Jews—although they are more lenient in their conclusions than the Orthodox—stay closer to traditional interpretation. An example of retaining tradition while adapting to modern times is the Conservative view of driving on the Sabbath. Orthodox Jews will not ride in an automobile on the Sabbath. Because of the spread-out nature of our communities, Conservative Judaism permits driving, but only to and from the synagogue. Reform Judaism, on the other hand, permit driving in an automobile on the Sabbath.

Reconstructionist Jews

The Reconstructionist Movement is the youngest of the major movements and is an outgrowth of the Conservative movement. It also has had an influence on the Reform Movement. Reconstructionists view Judaism as a civilization, and they call for the development of an organic Jewish community which will represent all Jews. They seek to revitalize the Jewish religion, defining God as the Power that makes for the realization of the best in one's self and in all people.

Reconstructionists do not believe that the Jews are the Chosen People. They also promote the cultivation of drama, music, dance, sculpture and the graphic arts as important elements for Jewish growth. In recent years the movement has become more spiritualy rooted, placing the *Divine Wisdom* at its center.

While the majority of the Jews in the United States, either identify with, or belong to one of these different religious groupings, we all tend to work together in our community and charity endeavors. In cities with a Jewish community there usually is a Jewish Federation or council which helps to coordinate Jewish activities on local, national and international levels.

✡

Chapter Two
The Jewish People Believe in God

THE DECLARATION WHICH WE, AS JEWS, USE TO SUM UP OUR FAITH is called the *Sh'ma*. The *Sh'ma* is the watchword of the Jewish People. It comes from the Bible and is found in the fifth of the *Five Books of Moses*, known as *Deuteronomy*. *Deuteronomy* 6:4 reads: *Sh'ma Yisrael, Adonai Elohenu, Adonai Echad'* —"Hear, O Israel: the Lord our God, the Lord is One."*

The history of the *Sh'ma* goes far back into biblical times. The *Torah* tells us that, after crossing the Red Sea and escaping from their enslavement in Egypt, our ancesters spent forty years wandering in the desert. When the time came to cross over the Jordan River and enter the land of Canaan, which today is called Israel, Moses called the people together to review the commandments so that they might better practice them in their new home.

Moses began his speech by exclaiming, "Hear, O Israel." (Israel is another name for the Jewish People.) He told them to listen to him, and then he talked about God, "*Adonai Elohenu, Adonai Echad* —The Lord our God, the Lord is One."

"The God of the Jewish People," he told them, "is *Adonai.*" The importance of *Adonai* is that there is but one *Adonai*, or Lord.

---

* See Glossary page 56 for new gender-sensitive translations.

Other people may worship many gods in the forms of idols of stone, wood, or even the trees of the forest, but the Jewish People are to worship *Adonai*, or the Lord, who is the One God.

While the Bible describes how Moses assembled the people to tell them about *Adonai*, many modern Jews believe that this story did not happen exactly as the Bible describes. Long after the Jewish People had settled in the land of Canaan, some began worshipping the idols of their neighbors on the tops of hills or under especially beautiful trees. These places were called shrines. However, the Jewish religious leaders did not approve of these practices. They wanted the people to worship the One God— not pagan statues and images.

Many current scholars believe that these ancient Jewish leaders collected many of the older laws and Jewish traditions and added some new ones. They brought them all together in what we call the *Book of Deuteronomy*. Thus, we read in the Bible that Moses called the people together and said unto them: *Sh'ma Yisrael, Adonai Elohenu, Adonai Echad* —"Hear, O Israel: the Lord our God, the Lord is One." By speaking through the name of Moses, the leaders impressed upon the people that the proper setting in which to worship God was in the Temple in Jerusalem— and not in any place, nice as it might be, where the neighboring peoples worshipped their idols.

Since Moses' time, we have come to understand that God can be worshipped in every city and place in the world, as well as in Jerusalem. Thus, George Washington was able to find Haym Salomon praying in a synagogue in Philadelphia. However, in Biblical days our ancesters believed that God should be worshipped in the Temple in Jerusalem. This change of emphasis from Jerusalem to the local synagogue will be better understood as we read on.

Whether one accepts the first or the second interpretation of the story, the importance of the biblical account is very clear. The Jewish leaders wanted the people to know that while some people may worship idols, Jews have but one God.

This God cannot be seen nor is there anything like God in the sky, nor on the earth, nor in the waters under the earth. Judaism hold that God is One.

In time, the *Sh'ma* was included in the Jewish prayerbook. In fact, many passages in the our prayerbook were taken directly from the Bible. The Bible contains poems and songs which we use as prayers to God. The rabbis and teachers who wrote the prayerbook respected the Bible so much that they used these prayers as their own.

Some Jewish historians believe that the Ten Commandments, found originally in the *Torah* (Exodus 20:1-14 and Deuteronomy 5:2-18) were put into the prayerbook and placed next to the *Sh'ma*. The first commandment clearly states, "*I am the Lord your God . . . Do not have any other gods before me.*" Today, however, the Ten Commandments are no longer found in this position.

In ancient Canaan our ancestors lived among many different peoples who believed there were numerous gods instead of just one God. These people tried to influence the Jews to give up their belief in the Lord Who is One and to worship their many gods instead. Our leaders, however, were always careful to preserve the teaching about the Oneness of God. They used the story of Moses to inspire the people with loyalty to the One God.

Later, when our ancestors where exiled to Babylonia and Persia after the destruction of the First Temple, they encountered the Zoroastrian religion which was founded on a belief in just two, rather than in many, gods. These two gods ruled the world: the God of Light or Good, and the God of Darkness or Evil. At the same time, our prophet Isaiah—a great and wise teacher—taught us that God is both the God of good and of evil, and that the *Adonai* of the *Sh'ma* was the one God of the whole world and the Creator of everything. To Isaiah, *Adonai* was the God of the Jewish People, of the Babylonian and Persian people, and of all the other peoples of the earth.

When Christianity came into the world, the Christians taught that there are three distinct forms to the One God:

1. God the Father;

2. God the Son--God appeared on the earth in the form of his only begotten son, Jesus, and also as the promised Messiah;

3. God the Holy Spirit--the Spirit of God which is visited upon believers from the time of the first Christian Pentecost.

God existing in three forms is known to Christians as the Doctrine of the Trinity.

Christians tried to convince the Jews that the Christian idea of God was the "true" one. They said that they, too, believed in the Ten Commandments, and that the God of the Ten Commandments was also the God of the Trinity.

The Rabbis then placed more focus upon the *Sh'ma* then the Ten Commandments. They taught that the Oneness of God was the most important idea in Judaism, regardless of what people of other new religions might say. To this day Jews believe that God is One—there is only one God. The Ten Commandments, however, remain basic to Judaism and are universally accepted as one of the greatest gifts of the Jewish People to civilization.

The *Sh'ma* declares that since there is only one God in the entire world, the physical laws by which the world works are the same everywhere. When an airplane takes off at a given altitude in the United States, the amount of speed which the plane must reach before its wheels can leave the ground, is exactly the same as if this very airplane were taking off at the same altitude in any other part of the world. It does not matter whether one is talking about an automobile, an airplane, a computer or a fiber-optics communication network—the physical laws by which the world operates are the same laws for every place and for every person.

Traditionally, a Jew is obligated to obey not just the Ten Commandments, but all the laws of the *Torah*, as interpreted by the Rabbis.

A non-Jew is called upon to obey at least what the Rabbis call the *Seven Laws of Noah:*

1. Not to deny God (ie. idolatry)
2. Not to blaspheme God
3. Not to murder
4. Not to engage in incestuous, adulterous, bestial relationships
5. Not to steal
6. Not to eat the limb torn from a living animal
7. To set up courts to ensure obedience to the other six laws.

(Talmud-Sanhedrin 56a)

The *Sh'ma* asserts that all people everywhere are the children of the same God. Another of our great prophets of biblical times, the prophet Malachai, interpreted the meaning of the *Sh'ma* in these words: *"Have we not all one father? Has not one God created us?"* (Mal. 2:10)

The Rabbis of the *Talmud* told the story of a man who wanted to coin money. First he made a die, and from this die he pressed out the coins. When he looked at them, he noticed that every one of the coins was exactly alike. Using this parable—which in Hebrew is called a *Midrash*, or interpretation—the Rabbis explained that when God wanted to make people on this earth, He first made a die, namely the first man. Then He made all the other people of the earth according to this pattern. However, when God looked at all the human beings, He noticed that even though He used the same pattern for all of them, each one looked different.

"How wonderful is the work of God," said the Rabbis. For them, God is the Father of all people, and yet each individual is treated as an important person.

The Messiah

The concept of a *Messiah* played an important part in the development of Judaism. There are two interpretations in Jewish tradition: 1) A personal *Messiah*, and 2) A Messianic Age.

Today, Orthodox Jews continue to believe in a personal *Messiah*. When that *Messiah* comes, the Temple will be rebuilt in Jerusalem and the priesthood will be restored.

Most Reform and Reconstructionist Jews prefer to speak of a Messianic Age. They believe that the priesthood is a thing of the past; therefore, all references, except as history, are eliminated from the Reform prayerbook. The Conservative prayerbook also retains many prayers about the priests for the sake of tradition.

Reform and Reconstructionist Jews view the hope of Messianic redemption more as a blueprint for human action and in opposition to the holocausts of history rather than as hope for divine miraculous intervention.

✡

Historical Time Line

c. 1800 B.C.E.	Abraham and Sarah	The *Tanach*—
c. 1300 B.C.E.	Moses and Sinai	The Biblical
586 B.C.E.	Destruction of the First Temple by the Babylonians	Period
c. 200 B.C.E.	Beginning of the Rabbis	

∞

32 C.E.	Approximate Date of Death of Jesus	The *Talmud*—
70 C.E.	Destruction of the Second Temple by the Romans	The Talmudic
c. 200 C.E.	The *Mishna* is Written Down	Period
c. 550 C.E.	The *Gemara* is Written Down	

∞

c. 1000 C.E.	Babylonian Scholarship Ends	*Responsa*
1492 C.E.	Spanish Golden Age Ends	*Literature*

∞

19th Century	Reform, Modern-Orthodox and Conservative Movements Begin
1897 C.E.	Birth of Zionism with the Goal of a New Jewish State
1948 C.E.	Founding of the Modern State of Israel

∞

Some dates on this chart are rounded off to the nearest century.

∞

Chapter Three
The Jewish People Believe in the Bible

THE JEWISH PEOPLE ARE CALLED THE *PEOPLE OF THE BOOK*, a name given to them by Mohammed, the founder of the Islamic religion. The *Book* is the Bible—*Tanakh*—the Holy Scriptures of the Jewish People. The Bible is a sacred book, containing the laws upon which Jewish life has been established. In its pages are recorded the revelations of God, the prophets, the kings, the scribes, and the sages of ancient Israel. The Bible tells the story of how God and the ancient Hebrews entered into a covenant and describes the laws and way of life which we and our descendants were to follow as the people of God.

The history of the Bible goes back to the beginning of Jewish life, nearly 4,000 years ago. At first the story of what God meant to the Jewish People was handed down by word of mouth from parent to child. Eventually these experiences and teachings were written down.

Though written many centuries ago, the Bible is a very contemporary book. The ancient Jewish ideals of justice, love, mercy, peace, and brotherhood are still important for us today. For example, when the founders of our country wanted a seal for the new republic, they first proposed as their theme the biblical story of the crossing of the Red Sea by the children of Israel. (see page 12.) Even now, when men and women are in trouble, many still turn for comfort to the Twenty-third Psalm, (the Twenty-second Psalm in the Catholic Bible), or to other Biblical readings. Even now, Jews read a portion of the Bible each week in their synagogues.

The English term Bible stems from the Greek, *Biblio* meaning, *book*. The Bible is a collection or library of many books. The Jewish Bible, which also is refered to as the Hebrew Scriptures, is what Christians call the *Old Testament*. The Jewish Bible does not contain the *New Testament*. Just the same, we Jews always regard and refer to our Holy Scripture as the Bible.

The Christian Bible contains both the *Old Testament* and the *New Testament*. The *New Testament* is a record of the life and teachings of Jesus and his followers. The use of the word "new" implies that the *New Testament* has come to complete the *Old Testament*. For Christians, therefore, the Bible contains both testaments.

What Christians call the *Old Testament* and what Jews consider to be the complete Bible are substantially the same. In the Christian *Old Testament* the names of the books sometimes have different forms than they do in the Jewish Bible. Also the order of the books is somewhat different. Catholics add an *Apocrypha*—books and parts of books which are not found in the Jewish Bible. These extra books were collected originally by Jewish scholars who lived in Alexandria, Egypt. When the early Church compiled its Bible, it also included this collection. The Catholic Church considers these books to be just as much a part of their Scripture as the other thirty-nine books of the Bible. We Jews, on the other hand, use these additional books only to shed light on the history and thought of Jewish life as our ancestors lived nearly 2,000 years ago.

The Bible *(Tanakh)*

The Jewish Bible is divided into three parts:

1. The *Torah,* or the *Five Books of Moses.*
2. The *Prophets* which are divided into the Early and the Later Prophets
3. The *Writings,* which are divided into the Wisdom Literature, the Five Scrolls, and the Historical Books.

It is particularly important that you remember the name of the first part, the *Torah.* We will speak of it many times.

It took nearly a thousand years to write the Jewish Bible. The earliest parts of the Bible (as we have it now) can be dated back to almost 2,000 years <u>before</u> Jesus was born. It was over one hundred years <u>after</u> Jesus was born that the Rabbis decided which of these ancient books to canonize as the Bible.

While there are thirty-nine books by count in the Jewish Bible, Jewish tradition records only twenty-four. The reason for this is that all of the "first" and "second" books (ie. *First Samuel* and *Second Samuel*) are counted as one. The *Twelve Prophets* count as one book, and *Ezra* and *Nehemiah* together also count as one book. The division into the "first" and "second" books came about because an early printer who lived in the Middle Ages divided the very long Biblical books in order to make them easier to produce.

The difference between the Early Prophets and the Later Prophets rests, for us, in the fact that the actual writings of the Later Prophets were preserved. The books of the Early Prophets contain only stories about them. Also, we do not refer to the *Twelve Prophets* as the minor prophets, nor to *Isaiah, Jeremiah,* and *Ezekiel* as the major prophets. Some of the most important teachings in Judaism are to be found in the writings of the twelve smaller prophetic books. The terms "major" and "minor" were attached to our prophets by the Christian world. The reason was not because of their importance but because of their length.

The Biblical *Book of Isaiah,* the *Book of Jeremiah,* and the *Book of Ezekiel* have sixty-six, fifty-two, and forty-eight chapters, respectively, and were considered to be "major" works in terms of length. On the other hand, the *Twelve Prophets* have from one to fourteen chapters each and are, relatively speaking, "minor" works in terms of length.

The Laws and Commandments *(Mitzvot)* of the Bible

The laws of the Bible form the basis upon which Jewish life has developed. In today's terms, many people think that some Biblical laws were very harsh. They point to the passage in the *Book of Exodus* which says: *"An eye for an eye, a tooth for a tooth ... ."* (Exodus 21:24) Actually, this biblical law was a significant improvement over the harsher laws of other people.

The accepted laws of the major surrounding civilizations said that if a man [of a lower class] caused another man to lose his eye, or even his tooth, he should be put to death. The biblical writers thought that this law was inhumane and that civilized people should not take a human life for such reasons. Thus our Bible states that only an eye should be taken for an eye. Later, the Jewish sages changed the Biblical law, so that money should be paid to the injured party for the loss of an eye or a tooth. This practice is followed today under the civil laws of the United States.

By reading parts of the Jewish Bible, we can learn about some of the laws which the Jewish People and Jesus himself followed.

Good examples are found in the *Book of Leviticus*, Chap. 19:

You shall not steal; neither shall you deal falsely, nor lie one to another. (19:11)

You shall not oppress your neighbor, nor rob him; the wages of a hired servant shall not abide with you all night until the morning. (19:13)

You shall not curse the deaf, nor put a stumbling-block before the blind, but you shall fear your God: I am the Lord. (19:14)

You shall do no unrighteousness in judgment; you shall not respect the person of the poor, nor favor the person of the mighty; but in righteousness shall you judge your neighbor. (19:15)

You shall not go up and down as a talebearer among your people; neither shall you stand idly by the blood of your neighbor: I am the Lord. (19:16)

You shall not hate your brother in your heart; you shall surely rebuke your neighbor, and not bear sin because of him. (19:17)

You shall not take vengeance, nor bear any grudge against the children of your people, but **you shall love your neighbor as yourself:** I am the Lord. (19:18)

Judaism gave to the world the teaching *"Love your neighbor as yourself."* Jesus, in making this Jewish statement one of his great commandments, followed teaching of the Jewish Bible.

The Talmud

The Bible is not the only Scripture holy to the Jewish People. The *Talmud*, too, is part of our sacred literature. After the Bible was completed, many new Jewish laws were developed. Sometimes the biblical laws were defined further to give them new meaning. The discussions which the Rabbis held were very similar to those which the Justices of the Supreme Court of the United

States conduct today when they try to interpret the laws of the Constitution. The Justices debate until they come to a clearer understanding of the law, and then they render their decision. In the same way, our early Rabbis debated the laws of the Bible until a decision was reached. These decisions were then taught to the people.

Whenever new laws are necessary, rabbis also act in a way which is similar to the Congress of the United States. In Congress whenever our lawmakers discuss new ideas, they try to make the final legislation agree with the principles of the Constitution. The constitution for our ancient Rabbis was the *Torah*. Therefore, whenever our Rabbis created a new law, or new interpretation of an older law, they were careful to make sure it was in keeping with the basic teachings of the *Torah*, which they regarded as perfect and permanent. In time, these new interpretations of the old laws, as well as the new laws themselves, were brought together in a collection of books called the *Talmud*.

It took our Rabbis a long time to create the *Talmud*. The process began nearly 200 years before Jesus was born. It was completed over five hundred years after his death. The *Talmud* covers nearly seven hundred years of Jewish history and was completed in two stages.

The first stage of completion was around 200 C.E. when the interpretations and new laws in existence since the completion of the Bible were collected into the *Mishnah*. The *Mishnah* contains 63 different books divided into six "orders," or main parts. About 550 C.E. the second phase was completed with the collection of all new interpretations and laws since the time of the *Mishnah*. This second series of writings which further interprets the laws of about half the books of the *Mishnah,* is known as the *Gemara.*

The *Talmud* represents the combined writings of the *Mishnah* and the *Gemara.* The *Talmud* is so arranged that each paragraph of the *Mishnah* is followed by the portion of the *Gemara* which forms its interpretation.

The *Talmud* contains not only laws and interpretations but also many beautiful stories that our Rabbis added to help explain the laws to us. To teach that one's wrongdoings affect not only one's self, Rabbi Shimon ben Yochai said:

> A number of men were seated in a boat, and one of them took an auger and began boring a hole beneath him. His comrades exclaimed: "What are you doing there?"
>
> He replied, "What concern is it of yours? Am I not boring a hole beneath my own seat?"
>
> They replied: "Surely it is our business, for the water will swamp the boat and all of us with it."   —*Midrash*

And again:

> There are four types of people: the one who says, "What is mine is mine, and what is yours is yours"--the usual type; the one who says, "What is mine is yours, and what is yours is mine"--the ignorant type; the one who says, "What is mine is yours and what is yours is yours"--the saintly type; the one who says, "What is yours is mine, and what is mine is mine—the evil type.
>
> —*Sayings of the Fathers*

This *Talumdic* method of teaching remains important today as we continue to question how ancient laws and traditions can be more meaningful to our lives.

✡

HEBREWS ✡ ISRAELITES ✡ JEWS

Some scholars believe that the name Hebrews came from the *Habiru,* wandering semi-nomads who lived in the Fertile Crescent stretching from Mesopotamia to Egypt, The Hebrews may have pronounced the name *Habiru* as *Ivri.* The Bible traces the term *Ivri to Eber,* a legendary ancestor (Gen. 11.16), Later, the term *Ever* means "the other side of"—presumabiy the Euphrates River—thus linking the name Hebrews with Abraham who came from Mesopotamia (Gen, 14,13),

✡

After Mt, Sinai, the Hebrews were called Israelites. They took tribal names (e.g., Judah, Ephraim) and also became united under the name of their common ancestor, *Israel,* the biblical Jacob, grandson of Abraham,

✡

The name Jew is of Greek origin. When Alexander the Great captured Jerusalem in 332 B.C.E., the Greek word *Ioudaios* was used to describe a "descendent of Judah." Under the Romans, the name became the Latin *Iudaeus,* In Old French, it was *Giu* and in Middle English Jeu.

✡

In modern day Israel, Jews, like all other citizens, are called Israelis to distinguish them from Jews who live in other countries.

✡

Chapter Four
The Jewish Holy Days & Festivals

The Jewish Calendar

THE JEWISH CALENDAR IS VERY ANCIENT. In early Jewish history the people were shepherds living in desert areas. Because it was hot during the day, they fed their flocks and traveled at night. The Jewish Calendar, therefore, was based upon the moon and is called a lunar calendar.

Each month in this calendar is 29-1/2 days long. This is the period of time that it takes for the moon to travel around the earth. Since a day cannot be divided in half, some months were given 29 days and others 30 days.

When the Jewish People settled in the land of Canaan, many became farmers. They soon noted that the seasons of the year were based upon the sun and not the moon. Today we know that it takes 365-1/4 days for the earth to make a complete revolution around the sun. As a result, a sun year is a little more than eleven days longer than a moon year. While our ancestors did not understand all these things, they did realize that before too long, using their lunar calendar, they were celebrating Spring holidays in the middle of Winter, and Fall festivals in Summer.

Recognizing that the farming of the crops depended upon the seasons according to the sun, the leaders adjusted their lunar calendar fit the seasonal cycle. Instead of adding, as is done today, one day every four years for a leap year, they added an entire month seven different times during a period of nineteen years. Thus, some years in the Jewish Calendar have thirteen months—*Adar I* and the added *Adar II*.

The Jewish Calendar counts the years according to the traditional date of the creation of the world. The *First Book of Chronicles* in the Bible lists the family tree of the Jewish People from Adam and Eve. By counting the time in which each person lived, our Rabbis established the date of Creation.

According to Jewish tradition the world was created on New Year's Day—*Rosh Hashanah*. The present year 1996-97 is the Jewish year 5757, and 1997-98 is the Jewish year 5758. Today most Jews accept that the world is much older, perhaps billions and billions of years older. Nevertheless, we still count the Jewish Calendar in the traditional way, even though we may interpret the Creation story in different ways.

Current Christian scholars recognize that, when their system of counting the years was begun a mistake was made regarding the date of the birth of Jesus. They believe Jesus was actually born four years before the date that has been chosen as the beginning of the Christian calendar. Even though this dating error is known, everyone continues to count the years in the traditional manner rather than adjusting records of the past two thousand years.

The Jewish calendar day begins with the appearance of three stars in the evening and ends at sunset the following day. The

Book of Genesis, (1:5), concerning the creation of the world, reads: *"And there was evening and there was morning, one day."* Since evening is mentioned first, the Jewish day begins with evening. All Jewish holidays likewise begin at sundown. It is important to remember this when consulting a Jewish Calendar.

On the following page is a listing of the dates of the Jewish holidays. The first one is the Sabbath which begins at sunset every Friday evening and ends when the sun goes down the following day. The other holidays come but once a year and fall on different days of the week. However, they all begin with sunset of the evening before the calendar date and end when the sun goes down the following day, or, with longer festival holidays, on sundown of the last calendar day.

The Jewish holy days may be divided into four groups as shown on the chart on the following page.

The Jewish Calendar also includes the following three days:

Tu B'shvat, or Jewish Arbor Day, usually falls in January, and is marked by the planting of trees. It is known as the New Year of the trees.

Lag B'Omer is the thirty-third day between Passover-*Pesach*—and Pentecost—*Shavuot.* It commemorates the heroic defense of the Jewish way of life by the Jews against the Romans in the first centuries of the Common Era.

Basic Jewish Holidays

Name of Holiday	Starting Hebrew Date	Corresponding Solar Date	Number of Days Celebrated
Sabbath The *Shabbat*		Friday evening to Saturday evening	Weekly 1 day
High Holy Days New Year or *Rosh Hashanah*	Tishri 1*	September or early October	Orthodox and Conservative, 2 days; Reform, 1 or 2 days
Day of Atonement or *Yom Kippur*	Tishri 10*	September	1 day
Pilgrim Festivals Passover or *Pesach*	Nisan 15 *	End of March or in April	Orthodox and Conservative, 8 days; Reform, 7 days
Pentecost or *Shavuot*	Sivan 6*	Middle May or early June	Orthodox/ Conservative, 2 days; Reform, 1 day
Tabernacles or *Sukkot/* ending with *Simchat Torah*	Tishri 15*	End of September or early October	Orthodox and Conservative, 9 days; Reform, 8 days
Victory Holidays Festival of Lights or *Chanukah*	Kislev 25 *	End of November or December	8 days
Feast of Lots or *Purim*	Adar 14*	February or March	1 day

* Starts the evening before

Tishah B'Av is the fast on the ninth day of the Hebrew month of Av, falling usually in early August and commemorating the destruction of both the First and Second Temples in Jerusalem.

Three additional observances have entered the Jewish Calendar because of Twentieth Century events:

Yom Hashoah, observed on the twelfth day between Passover and *Shavuot*, is the Holocaust Remembrance Day, recalling the six million Jews who were murdered by the Germans and their collborators during World War II.

Israel Independence Day falls on the fifth day of the Hebrew month of Iyar, which is either in April or May. It commemorates the establishment of the State of Israel in 1948.

Yom Yerusalayim, occurring just before *Shavuot* or the Pentecost, marks the establishment of Jerusalem as a united city following the Six Day War in 1967.

The Sabbath *(or the Shabbat)*

Sabbath is a most important holy day in Jewish life. Unlike the annual holy days or holidays, it falls on the seventh day of every week, beginning on Friday evening at sundown. It is then that we welcome the Sabbath—*Shabbat*—into our homes as though the day itself were a queen or a bride. This is a special day. Tradition tells us that on the Sabbath an extra soul—*Neshamah Yeterah*—descends from Heaven to join each Jew. It is as if the strength of a second person were added so that we can observe the Sabbath in greater beauty and holiness.

The Sabbath is observed in a threefold pattern:

1. a time for prayer to God in the home and the house of worship;

2. a time for special study of Jewish texts;

3. a day of renewal, different from the routine of the week.

Though Orthodox, Conservative and Reform Jews each interpret these aspects in different ways, the following practices are observed in Orthodox, Conservative and Reform Jewish homes.

As the sun sets, the mother kindles the Sabbath candles and officially welcomes the Sabbath queen or bride with a prayer. The glow of the candles twinkles happily in her eyes, and all of the members of the family feel warm and good. In Orthodox and some Conservative homes the men are attending *shul* for a short evening service while the women and children finish preparations for the Sabbath meal. The men return, and family and guests are together to share the Sabbath evening meal and festivities.

In other Conservative and in Reform homes the candles are lit with the entire family together and the Sabbath meal follows. After the meal, many of the families attend synagogue services while others continue to celebrate together at home.

The Sabbath is a time of thanksgiving. Father lifts a cup of wine and recites the sanctification blessing—*Kiddush*. The family expresses its gratitude for all the good things that have come into their lives since the last Sabbath. In the *Kiddush* prayer, the observance of the Sabbath is related to two important historic events in Judaism—the Exodus from Egypt and the creation of the world.

Then the entire family recites the blessing over the bread, called the *Motzi*, showing appreciation for the bounty of God's world. Father takes a piece of special Sabbath bread—*challah*—and shares it with each member of the family. *Challah* is usually an egg bread with rolling twists on top, baked especially for this occasion. This prayer also is used at all other meals during the week as grace before meals—*Blessed is the Lord our God, Ruler of the Universe, who causes bread to come forth from the earth.*

Traditionally it was customary for the father to bless the children. In many homes today both parents participate in this custom. Just as God is One, so also the Jewish family is "one," especially during Sabbath.

After dinner many Conservative and Reform families bring the Sabbath queen or bride as their guest to synagogue. This time, the Sabbath candles are lit with the entire congregation and the *Kiddush* is recited. The congregation prays and thanks God for the days of work , study and joy. We thank God for the Sabbath and for family. We also remember loved ones who died, and we pray for the health of the sick. The prayers are both personal and group oriented.

When the service ends, everyone wishes each other *Gut Shabbos* or *Shabbat Shalom*, "a good Sabbath." Usually refreshments follows the service in a gathering known as an *Oneg Shabbat*—the "Joy of the Sabbath."

On the Sabbath, the Bible is read in every synagogue. For each Sabbath a special portion of the *Torah* is assigned, as well as a passage taken either from the *Prophets* or the *Writings*, known as the *Haftarah*.

It takes a full year to read through the entire *Torah*. In addition, many Jews attend study classes on Saturday to learn about the Bible, the *Talmud,* and the many other sacred books of Judaism.

When twilight comes on Saturday evening, it is time for the Sabbath queen or bride to depart for another week. It is *Havdalah* time, or the "separation" of the Sabbath from the week-to-come. We say a blessing over a cup of wine. We pass a spice box from hand to hand, its sweet smell a reminder of the Sabbath that has just ended. We kindle a braided candle, generally with six wicks—one wick for each day of the coming week. As the six-fold flame is gently doused in the cup of wine, everyone bids the Sabbath farewell and wishes the members of the household and friends a *Shavua Tov,*—"a good week."

The High Holy Days

The New Year and the Day of Atonement

Judaism emphasizes the idea of repentance: we can admit wrongdoings and change our ways to overcome the wrong. The Bible tells us that God does not delight in the death of the wicked. Rather God desires that they turn from their evil ways and live. (Ezek. 33:11)

In order to give us an opportunity to correct our wrongdoings and to better our ways in this world, the religious calendar of Judaism has set aside ten important days each year. These are the High Holy Days, beginning with the New Year—*Rosh Hashanah*—usually in September and concluding ten days later with the Day of Atonement—*Yom Kippur.*

To illustrate the importance of repentence, a Jewish tradition tells us that, on the New Year Day, God sits on His throne, and before Him there are two books. The first book is called the *Book of Life,* and in its pages God writes the names of all people whose deeds of the past year qualify them for life during the coming year. The second book is called the *Book of Death* in which God records the names of all people who, because of their transgressions, deserve to die during the coming year.

However, God leaves the fate of the second group open until the Day of Atonement. God waits ten days for us to correct our wrongs before "inscribing and sealing" our names either in the *Book of Life* or the *Book of Death.*

The *Talmud* teaches us that there are two kinds of wrong-doings. (*Mishnah Yoma* 8.9): The wrongdoings between a person and God, and the wrongdoings between one person and another.

1. **Between a person and God.** God has given to every person a threefold gift—the power to grow physically, intellectually and emotionally. If we do not take care of our bodies, if we do not develop our intellectual capacities, and if we do not understand and manage our feelings, we are committing a wrong between ourselves and God.

    As we recognize our errors and agree to take care of these three wonderful gifts, God will hear our prayers and forgive our wrongdoings.

    The Jewish tradition also interprets the wrongs between people and God to mean our failure to carry out the rituals which God requires of us as Jews.

2. **Between one person and another.** God has given us a
fourth gift: the ability to relate to other people. If we do not
get along with others, or if we hurt someone by our actions
or words, God will not forgive us even if we pray to God
hard and long.

Before we may be forgiven, we must go to those whom we
have wronged and right that wrong. Then our *Talmud* adds
God will hear our prayers and forgive us. In personal
matters, God will accept our vows to change. But where
these promises affect another person, God wants us first to
correct our wrong-doings with the other person before we
can be forgiven by God.

As Jews, we listen to the sounds of the *shofar,* or the curved
ram's horn, in the synagogue on *Rosh Hashanah,* to remind us to
right the wrongs that we have committed before *Yom Kippur*
arrives in ten days. The *shofar* is sounded again to close *Yom
Kippur*—Day of Atonement—services.

The Three Pilgrim Festivals

Americans are proud of the small group of Pilgrims who came
to this country in 1620 to seek religious freedom. We Jews
remember still another group of pilgrims. These are the Jewish
men and women who lived thousands of years ago in ancient
Palestine. The name Palestine is derived from the name "Philistines," in Hebrew *P'lishtim.* Scholars believe the Philistines
entered the Land of Canaan from the Mediterranean Sea shortly
after the time of Joshua in the 12th century B.C.E. Today, the
name "Israel" is used for the Jewish State, and the name
"Palestine" is used for the general area, as well as for a specific
territory that is becoming a new Arab administered territory.

In ancient Palestine our ancestors would make a pilgrimage three times a year to the Temple in Jerusalem bringing their offerings to God. The first pilgimage came at the beginning of the spring planting season, at Passover—*Pesach* and involved the sacrifice of the *Pascal* lamb as well as a feast of the lamb that evening. The second visit was made seven weeks later when the first harvest had been reaped at Pentecost—*Shavuot*. The third pilgrimage came at the very end of the summer when the final harvest had been gathered and been brought in from the fields and orchards at Tabernacles —*Sukkot*. Thus Passover, Pentecost and Tabernacles *(Pesach, Shavuot and Sukkot)* are called the Three Pilgrim Festivals.

Passover (or Pesach)

Jews worldwide celebrate Passover as a holiday of springtime and as the commemoration of the escape of our ancestors from slavery in ancient Egypt. On the first night of Passover we gather together with our families for the *Seder* meal and read the story of the Exodus in the *Haggadah*—a special book prepared for the home service.

The word *Seder* means "order" and refers to the program and festive meal which is the focus of the holiday. The table is set with the finest linens and silverware, and in front of the leader's place is a beautiful *Seder* plate containing many symbolic foods. There is green parsley to remind us of the springtime when nature makes everything green again. The shank bone of the lamb recalls the sacrifice and eating of the *Pascal* lamb as our ancestors prepared to leave Egypt. The bitter herbs and the brown mixture of apples, nuts, cinnamon and wine called *charoset* are reminders of the Egyptian slavery and of the brownish bricks our forefathers made for Pharaoh. The salt water is a symbol of the tears of bitterness which our people shed in their bondage. Others say that the salt water refers to the waters of the Red Sea. The roasted egg symbolizes the Temple sacrifices and is a reminder to us of the new life that is possible for a free people.

A second plate containing three pieces of unleavened bread, called *matzah,* is placed on the table. The Bible tells us that this was the bread, made without a leavening agent such as yeast, which the Israelites baked in their haste to leave Egypt. At the *Seder* meal, one of the three pieces of *matzah* is broken in half, with one part being called the *afikomen. Afikomen* is a Greek word meaning dessert.

In order to keep the children awake during the *Seder ,* a game called "hiding the *afikomen"* is played. At dessert time the children look for it, and the finder receives a gift. During the *Seder* the *matzah* is also used to make a sandwich with the bitter herbs and *charoset.*

One of the highlights of the *Seder* meal is the asking of the *Four Questions.* First there is the general question, "Why is this night different from all other nights?" This gives the leader an opportunity to tell the story of our Exodus from Egypt, which is found in the *Haggadah,* and to respond to the *Four Questions* traditionaly asked by the youngest child:

1. On all other nights, we eat leavened bread and *matzah;* on this night, why do we eat only *matzah?*

2. On all other nights, we eat all kinds of herbs; on this night, why do we eat mainly bitter herbs?

3. On all other nights, we do not dip even once; on this night, why do we dip twice?

4. On all other nights, we eat either sitting straight or reclining; on this night, why do we all recline?

Four cups of wine are drunk by each participant at the *Seder* meal. At each *Seder* table there is also an extra place setting with an extra wine cup. The chair at this setting remains unoccupied, for this is the "fifth cup" reserved for Elijah the prophet. During the ceremony for Elijah, a child opens the door of the home in the hope that freedom—symbolized through Elijah's drinking from the cup—will come to all the Jewish People and to all humanity. Everyone watches the cup carefully to see if the wine deminishes in order to tell of Elijah's arrival.

The five cups of wine used in the *Seder* service symbolize the five phrases in Exodus 6:6-8 which describe God's promise to save the Jewish People from slavery in Egypt:

1. "I will bring you out;"

2. "I will deliver you;"

3. "I will redeem you;"

4. "I will take you to Me for a people" and

5. "I will bring you in unto the land."

Seder time is both a happy and a serious time for American Jews. Both the American and Jewish traditions remind us how important it is for people to be free from all kinds of slavery. The *Haggadah* teaches: "Let all who are hungry, come and eat." In the same way, the Liberty Bell in Independence Hall in Philadelphia is engraved with the words: *"Proclaim liberty throughout the land, unto all the inhabitants thereof"* (Lev. 25:10).

Pentecost (or Shavuot)

Jews celebrate the Pentecost—*Shavuot*— as the time of the gathering of the late spring harvest and as the time when Moses went up to the top of Mt. Sinai. There is the tradition that on Pentecost the Israelites received the Ten Commandments at Mt. Sinai. Although many Jews and Christians may not accept the literal details of the story of Moses on Mt. Sinai, they do respect and honor the teachings of the Ten Commandments: *"You shall honor your father and your mother ... You shall not murder ... You shall not steal ... etc."* (Exod 20:12-15). Pentecost is also the time of confirmation, when Jewish teenagers pledge their faith to the teachings of the *Torah*.

Christians are familiar with the name of Pentecost, which means *"fifty."* According to the *New Testament,* Jesus died at Passover time. In the Jewish Calendar, Pentecost is fifty days after Passover, and it is Christian belief that on the Pentecost following the death of Jesus, the Holy Spirit descended on the Apostles. Christians commemorate the descent of the Holy Spirit by the Greek name of the Jewish feast, Pentecost, because that is when they believe it occurred.

Tabernacles (or Sukkot)

Tabernacles—*Sukkot*—is the Jewish thanksgiving time. Many of us build a tabernacle or booth—*sukkah*—in our yards, in which we eat all our meals. The pulpit in the synagogue often is decorated with fruit and the walls of the tabernacle with the yellowing stalks of corn. Some of us build a miniature *sukkah* as a centerpiece for our festive tables at home.

These tabernacles or booths are reminders of the temporary houses in which the Israelites lived while traveling in the desert after their escape from Egypt. They are symbolic of the booths which our ancestors put in their fields during harvest season once they were settled in the land of Israel. Since the rains came early in the Fall in Palestine, the people spent the night in the fields in these little huts so that they would not have to waste time going back and forth from their homes each day.

In building the *sukkah*, the plants and the leaves which form the roof are not to be laid on too thickly so that the heavens and the stars are visible for "the heavens declare the glory of God." (Psalms 19.)

In celebration of Tabernacles, we wave a sweet smelling *etrog* or citron, which looks like a lemon, and a *lulav* containing three plants—myrtle, willow and palm branch—to the heavens above, to the earth beneath, to the east, to the west, to the north, and to the south. This ceremony reminds us that our blessings come from everywhere—from one God, Who is everywhere.

Sukkot time is not only a thanksgiving time but also a time for sharing. It is a modern tradition to take the fruit with which the tabernacle is decorated and give it to a needy family. Children in the religious school collect food which is distributed to charitable institutions. It is an old custom called *ushpizin* to invite friends and even strangers to be a guest and celebrate meals in the *sukkah*.

Following the last day of this third Pilgrim Festival, we celebrate the "Joy of the Torah"—*Simchat Torah*. The weekly readings from the *Five Books of Moses* which take one year to complete are finished on *Simchat Torah*. The *Torah* scroll is immediately rewound to the beginning or a second *Torah* scroll already rolled to the first passages from *Genesis* are read: *"In the beginning God................."*

Some congregations follow a three-year cycle, reading one third of the weekly *Torah* portion so that the entire *Torah* is read over a three year period. The celebration of *Simchat Torah,* however, is marked each year. On *Simchat Torah,* we parade proudly in our synagogues with the *Torah* scrolls. At this season of the year new religious school students also are consecrated as pilgrims of the *Torah.*

The Victory Holidays

Festival of Lights (or Chanukah)

Chanukah, or The Festival of Lights, is the Jewish holiday of religious freedom. Almost 2,200 years ago, after the death of Alexander the Great, a Greek-Syrian king tried to force all the Jews in Palestine to worship Greek idols instead of their One God. When the Syrians placed statues of Greek gods in the Holy Temple in Jerusalem, the Jews revolted under the leadership of a family called the Maccabees. After many years the Maccabees defeated the Syrians, the idols were removed and the Temple was reconsecrated. Once again the Jewish People were free to worship God as they chose.

The Maccabean heroes, through their fierce loyalty to Judaism, gave to the world the concept of religious freedom. When our American forefathers enacted the Constitution of the United States and the Bill of Rights, they included in it the spirit of the Maccabees. The First Amendment to the Constitution prohibits the government from establishing an official religion for its citizens.

As American Jews we are proud of our Maccabean ancestors. A tradition tells that the little vessel of oil which was supposed to burn for only one day in the Temple *menorah*, burned for eight days and became part of the miracle of *Chanukah*. On each of the eight nights of the *Chanukah* festival, lights are kindled in a special candleholder called a *chanukiah* or *Chanukah menorah* to recall the heroism of the Maccabees and the principle of religious freedom.

On the first night we kindle one candle, and each following night we add one more candle until on the eighth night eight candles and the serving candle, called the *Shammash*, burn brightly in our homes.

On the first night of *Chanukah*, three blessings also are recited. On all other nights just the first two blessings are used:

Blessed is the Lord our God, Ruler of the Universe, who hallows us with His *mitzvot*, (commandments) and commands us to kindle the *Chanukah* lights.

Blessed is the Lord our God, Ruler of the Universe, who performed wondrous deeds for our ancestors in days of old, at this season.

Blessed is the Lord our God, Ruler of the Universe, for giving us life, for sustaining us, and for enabling us to reach this season.

Chanukah is a very happy time for Jewish People. We eat potato pancakes, which are called *latkes*, and sing *Chanukah* songs. We exchange gifts and spin tops, called *dreidels*, with four Hebrew letters written on the sides.

With the *dreidel* tops Jewish boys and girls play a game of put-and-take. Each letter on the *dreidel* stands for a word. <u>N</u>un means *nisht* or "nothing." <u>G</u>immel means *gantz* or "all." <u>S</u>hin means *shtel* or "put." <u>H</u>ay means *halb* or "half." This game is played with nuts, raisins, pennies, or small candies. The players put one into the kitty to start the game. As the spinners take turns, they have to do what the *dreidel* tells them—put, take all, take half or do nothing. The game continues until there is no more in the kitty, and then the players start all over again.

The letters remind us of the Maccabean victory for religious freedom. *"Nes Gadol Hayah Sham*—A great wonder happened there."* These words refer to the victory of the tiny Maccabean army over the mighty soldiers of the Syrian king and the miracle of the oil that burned for eight days.

Feast of Lots (or Purim)

The Feast of Lots, known as *Purim* in Hebrew, is the story of beautiful Queen Esther, the wise Mordecai and the wicked Haman. *Purim,* however, is more than just an interesting story. This holiday teaches that other people's religious customs and laws should not be used as excuses to hate or hurt them.

In the Biblical *Book of Esther,* Haman, the prime minister of Persia, claimed that the rules of the Jewish People were different from those of the other Persian people. Therefore, he wanted King Ahasuerus to destroy all the Jewish People.

Haman's reason for disliking the Jews, however, was only an excuse. He was angry with Mordecai, who, in keeping with the teachings of his religion, refused to bow down before him. Although Mordecai respected the position of Prime Minister, he would not bow down before Haman, a human being.

No matter what plan Haman tried, he never succeeded in getting Mordecai to bow down before him. Moreover, every time Haman failed, he became angrier. Knowing Mordecai was

Jewish and believing the Jewish customs and laws were different from those of the Persians, Haman's wife concluded that Jews must be bad, and therefore, deserved to be destroyed. Haman followed his wife's suggestion and convinced the king to allow him to kill all the Jews.

Haman cast *lots*—*pur*—to decide on which day the Jews should be destroyed. However, his plot did not succeed. Queen Esther, the King's wife, who was Jewish, exposed Haman's scheme and saved her people.

Every year at *Purim*, we read the *Megillah of Esther*, which is the Biblical *Book of Esther* written in the form of a single scroll. We use noisemakers—*groggers*—to drown out the name of Haman whenever it is read. We enjoy three-cornered cakes — *hamantaschen*—filled with raisins or poppy seeds. The event is celebrated carnival-style with costume parties, a favorite of every Jew, young and old.

We are proud of our *Purim* holiday. We believe that the message of *Purim* is very important—that no one should be hated or hurt because the customs and laws of their religion are different from that of the society in which they live.

✡

Gender Sensitivity

Reform and Reconstructionist Judaism recently have become gender-sensitive in their prayers, leaving out gender references when it is possible. Conservative Judaism has been moving in the same direction but at a slower pace.

Gender-sensitive examples

Basic Blessing Introduction: *"Praised be our Eternal God, Ruler of the Universe. You hallow us with Mitzvot, (commandments) and command us ......"*

Blessing over Bread: *"Praised be our Eternal God, Ruler of the Universe, Who causes bread to come forth from the earth."*

Blessing the Shabbat Candles: *"Praised be our Eternal God, Ruler of the Universe, Who hallows us with Mitzvot and commands us to kindle the lights of the Sabbath."*

The *Barchu*, the Call to Worship: *"Praised be our Eternal God to Whom all praise is due forever and ever."*

The Sh'ma: "Hear, O Israel: the Eternal One is our God, the Eternal One alone!" **Line Following the *Sh'ma*:** *"Blessed is God's glorious Majesty forever and ever."*

Addition to the first lines of the *Amidah* prayer includes the four Matriarchs: *"and of the mothers, Sarah, Rebecca, Rachel and Leah."*

The Kiddush: *"Praised be our Eternal God, Ruler of the Universe, Creator of the fruit of the vine."*

The Closing Benediction:

> *"May God bless you and keep you.*
> *May God look kindly upon you and be gracious to you.*
> *May God reach out to you in tenderness and give*
>   *you peace."*

—Gates of Prayer for Weekdays, CCAR. 1993

Chapter Five
The Jewish House of Worship

TODAY IN AMERICA THERE ARE MANY BEAUTIFUL SYNAGOGUES displaying numerous architectural styles. Temple Emanu-El on New York's Fifth Avenue was built in early Romanesque design with tall, narrow stained glass windows. The Temple in Cleveland, Temple B'nai Jeshurun in Des Moines, Temple Sholom in Chicago, Temple Sinai and the Touro Synagogue in New Orleans, and Wilshire Boulevard Temple in Los Angeles all feature high domes in the Byzantine style. Temple Ohabei Shalom in Brookline, Massachusetts, has both a Byzantine and Romanesque design, while Temple Israel in Boston includes many ideas borrowed from the Temple of King Solomon in ancient Jerusalem. The high pillars of the Bene Israel Synagogue of Cincinnati are copied from Corinthian examples. Temple Israel of Lawrence, Long Island, combines a colonial appearance with a six-sided construction that outlines a Star of David when viewed from the air. Many of the newer buildings are modernistic in design. Congregation Shaarey Zedek in Detroit, Beth Sholom in Philadelphia, and Beth Tzedec in Toronto are examples of the newer architectural designs.

Some synagogues preserve very plain interiors. Congregation Shearith Israel in San Francisco and the Plum Street Temple in Cincinnati have brightly decorated sanctuaries. All Jewish houses of worship, however, whether they be Orthodox, Conservative or Reform, always contain the same central points of interest.

The Sanctuary

The Holy Ark and Eternal Light form the central focus of every synagogue. They correspond in location and importance to the Tabernacle in a Catholic church. The Crucifix in a Protestant church is placed in the same location as the Ark is in a synagogue.

The Holy Ark—*Aron Hakodesh*—is a cabinet located at the front of the sanctuary in which the *Torah* scrolls are placed. In some congregations a finely decorated mantle is hung in front of the Ark doors. Other congregations emphasize the beauty of the doors themselves. Sometime special sayings have been inscribed above the Ark doors. One oft-used inscription from the *Talmud* reads: *"Know before whom you stand."*

Although there are many ways to decorate the Ark and the Eternal Light, there is always an Ark and an Eternal Light in every Jewish house of worship.

The Eternal Light or *Ner Tamid* (Lev. 24:2) burns at all times and is placed above the Ark to indicate that God and the Jewish way of life are eternal.

In most synagogues there is a pulpit—*bimah*— for the rabbi and the cantor— near the center of the congregational seating area. In other congregations the pulpit area is in front of the Ark, but with the rabbi's lectern on one side and the cantor's on the other. The Ark and Eternal Light, however, are always placed at the front of the sanctuary.

At the side of the Ark there is a seven-branched candelabra —*menorah*. Very often, above the Ark, the tablets of the Ten Commandments are inscribed in Hebrew with the first two words of each of the commandments. Sometimes the Ten Commandments are inscribed on the doors of the Ark itself. Hebrew is written from right to left, and the First Commandment is on the right as one faces the tablets.

There also is a small pedestal to hold the candles which are lit in observance of the beginning of the Sabbath or a holiday and the *Kiddush* cup of wine. Often a colorful bouquet of flowers is placed on the pulpit to add to the beauty of the sanctuary.

In many Reform and Conservative synagogues choirs are used for the singing of hymns and chants. Sometimes the choir can be seen by the congregation. In other synagogues the choir sits in a loft where it is is heard but not seen. Most congregations have a cantor—*chazzan*—who sings and directs the music. In an Orthodox synagogue the melodies are sung without the accompaniment of musical instruments and with only the use of male voices.

There are many similarities between a synagogue and a Christian church. Since many of the first Christians were Jewish, the Christian Church quite naturally adapted many traditional Jewish symbols and rituals to their own needs. For example, in Catholic Churches, a sanctuary lamp is lit to signify the presence of the Blessed Sacrament in the tabernacle.

The Torah Scrolls

The *Torah* is housed within the Holy Ark. Since the *Torah* is a very sacred scroll to us, we often have several of them in the Ark.

Each scroll is identical in its contents, no matter what its size. On certain holidays special additional portions are read so that more than one scroll is used.

The *Torah* is written by hand with the use of a quill pen and a specially prepared ink upon a leather parchment. It takes the scribe—*sofer*—approximately three months to write a *Torah*. In Orthodox circles, the *sofer* is a man. In the liberal tradition a *Torah* can be written by any Jew who is trained in the skill of *Torah* writing.

First the *sofer* reads each word from a book; then he must pronounce the word aloud; finally, he writes it down. If he should make a mistake in a word, he can correct it; however, if he should misspell the name of God, he cannot erase the error. He must rewrite the entire page. The *Torah* is written in Hebrew, and the scribe writes only the consonants, leaving out all vowels and punctuation marks.

The ornaments of the *Torah* tell a very interesting story. During biblical times, the leader in the Holy Temple in Jerusalem, called the High Priest, wore special garments. On certain occasions he wore a crown upon his head and dressed in a flowing white gown with bells attached to the hemline. He also wore a breastplate which contained twelve brightly colored stones, representing the Twelve Tribes of Israel.

When the Second Temple was destroyed by the Romans shortly after Christianity emerged, the Jewish priesthood came to an end. The Rabbis then transferred the symbols of the clothes of the High Priest to the *Torah* scroll. The crown on the head of the High Priest became the crown of the *Torah*—the Crown of Learning. The bells were used as ornaments. The flowing white robe became the *Torah* cover—the mantle. The breastplate of the tribes became the breastplate decoration over the scroll. Today the *Torah* mantle itself is often decorated with these same symbols. Sometimes the Shield of David and Lions of Judah are added to these decorations.

To help a person in the reading of the *Torah* and to better preserve the ink and parchment, a pointer shaped like a finger was created. This pointer is called a *yad* which means "finger."

As we have noted earlier, a portion of the *Torah* is assigned for each week of the year and every year the reading of the entire scroll is completed. *Simchat Torah* is the time when we finish reading the *Book of Deuteronomy* and begin again with the *Book of Genesis*.

This practice of reading from the Scripture was carried over into the first half of the Catholic Mass, called the Liturgy of the Word. In Protestant churches Bible readings also form a major part of the service.

All synagogues use prayerbooks. Some are written entirely in Hebrew, while others have prayers both in Hebrew and in English. A prayer book is called a *siddur* in Hebrew. For the High Holy Days, *Rosh Hashanah* and *Yom Kippur*, a second prayer book, called a *machzor*, is used.

A Visit to a Synagogue

In Conservative and Orthodox congregations men wear a cap called a *yarmulkeh*, also known in Hebrew as a *kippah*. Usually it is available in a container at the entrance of the sactuary. In many Reform temples the wearing of a head covering is optional although most Reform rabbis and cantors wear one. Some women also cover their heads in a similar way.

In worshipping at an Orthodox synagogue, it is customary for the women to sit apart from the men. Often the balcony is set aside for the women worshippers. Men and women sit together in Reform and Conservative synagogues.

During some services Conservative and Orthodox men wear a prayer shawl—*tallit*—with specially knotted fringes on each of the four corners. During morning services, except on the Sabbath and holidays, they also wear the phylacteries— *tefillin*. These are little boxes containing portions of Scripture which are bound to the left arm and the forehead by means of leather straps. Both the *tefflin* and the fringes on the *tallet* remind us to dedicate our hearts and minds to the service of God. Although Reform Jews are not required to wear a *tallit* or put on *tefillin*, the wearing of the *tallit* by some of the men and even women has become more common.

During the Saturday morning service (and often in those Reform congregations where the *Torah* is read during the Friday night service) the men wear a *tallit*. Many Reform rabbis wear a *stole*, which resembles the prayer shawl, over their rabbinical gown. Many Conservative and Orthodox rabbis also wear black rabbinical gowns similar to those worn for graduation. However, during the High Holy Days, the gown is white.

Protocol for Guests

Visitors are always welcome in a synagogue. Guests should use the following procedures during the service:

1. Follow the appropriate practices with regard to head coverings and seating out of respect to the hosts.

2. Worship with the congregation, choosing to rise and to be seated with the congregation, or choose merely to observe, remaining seated at all times.

Jewish Prayer Services

In the Jewish tradition, morning, afternoon and evening prayer services are held each day. This practice still is followed in Orthodox and Conservative synagogues where the afternoon and evening services are held twenty minutes apart, just before and just after sunset. Although the Reform prayerbook contains three daily services, most Reform services are held primarily on the Sabbath, with an emphasis upon the Friday evening and the Saturday morning.

A Friday Evening Service

A Friday evening service in a Reform temple generally will have an order of service similar to the following:

1. The opening music
2. The kindling of the Sabbath lights
3. The call to worship and the prayers associated with the *Sh'ma*
4. The *Amidah,* concluding with silent devotion
5. The Sermon
6. The *Kiddush*
7. The Adoration
8. The *Kaddish*

9. The closing music

10. The Benediction

The opening music.

In some congregations, a period of silent prayer or meditation accompanied by music, will precede the service.

As the service opens, worshippers are greeted with Sabbath melodies. Some synagogues emphasize congregational singing, while others prefer to have the choir or the cantor, with or without choir and musical accompaniment, sing the hymns. There is a growing trend toward the combined use of cantors, choirs, and congregational singing.

The kindling of the Sabbath lights.

Following the opening music, a member of the congregation lights the Sabbath candles and inaugurates the Sabbath with the following prayer: *

> Blessed is the Lord our God, Ruler of the Universe, who hallows us with His *mitzvot,* (commandments) and commands us to kindle the lights of the Sabbath.
>
> May God bless us with Sabbath joy.
>
> May God bless us with Sabbath holiness.
>
> May God bless us with Sabbath peace.

The call to worship and the prayers associated with the Sh'ma.

After the candle blessings are completed, the formal prayer-book service begins. First there is an introductory prayer, concluded, in turn, by the Jewish call to worship. While it is

* See Glossary page 54 for new gender-sensitive translations.

customary for the rabbi to conduct the service, anyone who is learned in the procedure may do so. The rabbi, or one of the members of the congregation who becomes responsible for leading the service, calls the members to worship:

Praise the Lord, to whom all praise is due!

The congregation then responds:

Praised be the Lord to whom all praise is due forever and ever.

In Hebrew, the call to worship is known as the *Barchu*, meaning "Praise God."

Then the *Sh'ma*, the words affirming the unity of God, is repeated by the congregation:

Hear, O Israel, the Lord our God, the Lord is One.

After reciting the *Sh'ma*, we recall the words which the people recited in the ancient Temple in Jerusalem on the Day of Atonement as they stood before the High Priest:

Blessed is the name of His glorious kingdom for ever and ever.

While in the liberal congregations the worshippers stand to recite the *Sh'ma*, the more traditional practice is to recite it while seated.

This section of the service comes to a close with a prayer describing the Sabbath as a bond between the Jewish People and God. The Sabbath for the Jewish People is a day of rest, because, according to the Bible, God created the world in six days and rested on the seventh day. Therefore, the Sabbath has become a day of refreshment of the soul. For some of us this means stopping all kinds of work and devoting the Sabbath to prayer and study. For others, the Sabbath is a day of spiritual renewal or simple relaxation.

No matter which way we may interpret the seventh day, the Sabbath is a holy day in our Jewish calendar as described in the words of the Bible which the congregation sings:

> The children of Israel shall keep the Sabbath to observe the Sabbath through their generations for a perpetual covenant. It is a sign between Me and the children of Israel forever (Exodus 31:16-17).

The Amidah, concluding with silent devotion.

The word *Amidah* means "standing." In Orthodox and Conservative congregations the seven prayers of the *Amidah* are recited while the worshippers are standing. In Reform temples the congregation generally rises for the first three prayers. The first prayer praises God as the God of history—the God of the Biblical patriarchs Abraham, Isaac, and Jacob, and the Matriarchs Sarah, Rebekkah, Rachel and Leah. The second prayer speaks of God as the God of life. The third prayer speaks of God as the God of holiness.

Among the three closing prayers is one of our most beautiful, the *Prayer for Peace*. It describes our hope for universal peace among all people, when everyone will live in a relationship of justice and loving kindness with others. Frequently this version of the prayer is used:

> Grant us peace, your most precious gift, Eternal Source of Peace, and enable Israel to be its messenger unto the peoples of the earth. Bless our country that it may ever be a stronghold of peace, and its advocate in the council of nations. May contentment reign within its borders, health and happiness within its homes. Strengthen the bonds of friendship and fellowship among the inhabitants of all lands. Plant virtue in every soul, and may the love of Your name hallow every home and every heart. Blessed are You, Giver of Peace.

Between the opening and closing benedictions of the *Amidah* are special prayer dedicated to the Sabbath. Very often, rabbis also insert original prayers that are taken either from personal experience or from the events of the day.

The *Amidah* comes to a close with the silent prayer. For some of us it is a suggested psalm or word of wisdom from our teachers of old. For others, it is a new prayer which we have just created. We pray silently, each according to the way we feel, and then the choir closes with these words of Scripture:

> May the words of my mouth and the meditations of my heart be acceptable unto You, O Lord, my Rock and my Redeemer.
>
> (Psalm 19:15).

The Sermon.

The Sermon is the message given by the rabbi. Generally, it lasts from fifteen to thirty minutes. Depending upon the nature of the occasion, the sermon may explain a passage from Scripture, frequently the *Torah* portion. At other times, it takes the form of a lecture on a phase of Jewish history. Sometimes the sermon explains a thought or a current event. The rabbi often uses examples from the *Talmud* and the other sacred books of Judaism, as well from general literature, to illustrate the message of the sermon.

The Kiddush.

Wine in Jewish life is a symbol of joy, and we sanctify our joys through a blessing of thanksgiving known as the *Kiddush*. The singing of the *Kiddush* is usually led by the cantor, but often the husband of the one who has blessed the candles, or a congregant who is celebrating a special occasion will have the honor to lead the ceremony. Sometimes the *Kiddush* is celebrated at the end of the service and at the beginning of the *Oneg Shabbat*—the reception sponsored by the congregation or by individuals celebrating a special event.

> Blessed is the Lord our God, Ruler of the Universe, Creator of the fruit of the vine.

The Adoration.

Following the *Kiddush,* the Ark is opened and a prayer of adoration is recited. The worshippers say:

> Let us adore the ever-living God and . . . bow our heads in reverence . . . May the time not be distant . . . when superstition shall no longer enslave the mind, nor idolatry blind the eye, when all who dwell on earth shall know to You alone every knee must bend and every tongue give homage.

The Kaddish.

At each service we remember our departed loved ones through a prayer called the *Kaddish* or Sanctification. We do so in the spirit of the *Book of Job:* "The Lord gave, and the Lord has taken away." (1:21) In Judaism death is as natural as birth. While our hearts may be heavy, as mourners we try to continue in the spirit of Job: "Blessed be the name of the Lord." The *Kaddish* prayer is a call for courageous living when life itself often seems difficult. In many Reform congregations the worshippers rise as one and praise the name of God. In Orthodox and Conservative congregations only the mourners rise.

> Extolled and hallowed be the name of God throughout the world ... And may the kingdom of righteousness be established speedily on earth. Amen.

The Closing Benediction.

The service closes with the rabbi's benediction. Standing with hands raised, the rabbi often chooses the priestly blessing used by the High Priest in the ancient Temple in Jerusalem:

May the Lord bless you and keep you.
May the Lord let the light of His countenance shine upon you and be gracious unto you.
May the Lord lift up His countenance unto you and grant you peace.
(Num. 6:24-26).

After the benediction, the rabbi greets the congregation with the words of the Sabbath spirit: *Gut Shabbos,* "Good Sabbath," or *Shabbat Shalom,* "Sabbath Peace."

A Saturday Morning Service

In Orthodox synagogues the main emphasis is placed upon the Saturday morning service. On Friday evening, there is a service at sundown attended primarily by men. Then they return home for a family celebration of the Sabbath. More traditional Conservative worshippers also follow this same practice. In the more liberal Conservative and in Reform synagogues, a late Friday evening service is held after the home Sabbath dinner. On Saturday morning there is a Sabbath service. This is the service when boys become *Bar Mitzvah* and girls *Bat Mitzvah.*

A Saturday morning service at a Conservative synagogue will have the following order:

1. There is no candle lighting ceremony in the morning. Instead additional psalms and hymns for the Sabbath are added at the beginning of the service.

2. The prayers before and after the Call to Worship or the *Barchu* are adapted for a morning rather than an evening service. The *Sh'ma* is introduced by a much longer prayer and is followed by two sections found only on the Sabbath.

3. The *Amidah* is recited privately by each worshipper while standing.

4. The reading of the weekly portion of the *Torah* follows. It is usually divided into seven parts with an eighth part reserved for the person who later will read the *Haftarah*—a section from the *Prophets* or *Writings*. This eighth reading is called the *Maftir*. If there is a boy who is becoming a *Bar Mitzvah* this day, he will chant the *Maftir*. In some Conservative congregations this section may be chanted or read by a girl who is becoming a *Bat Mitzvah*. However, in more traditional Conservative synagogues the *Bat Mitzvah* chants only the *Haftarah*.

5. Following the *Torah* and *Haftarah* readings, the *Amidah* prayers are repeated out loud by the cantor and the congregation. This part of the service is called the *Musaf*. Again the congregation remains standing.

6. The service concludes with the Adoration, the *Kaddish* and with the singing of two hymns: *Ayn Kaylohenu*— There is None like Our God and *Adon Olam*—The Lord of All.

7. Different parts of the service are separated by the *Chatzi Kaddish* or the "Half-Kaddish" which is a shortened version of the complete *Kaddish* said at the end of the service. It is to be remembered that the *Kaddish*, generally known as the Mourner's Prayer, is entirely a praise of God. There is no mention in it of death or of the deceased. Therefore, it is

appropriate to use the *Chatzi Kaddish* with its praise of God for separating the different parts of the service.

8. The *Kiddush,* or the Sanctification over the wine, is recited or sung at the end of the service and forms part of the *Oneg Shabbat.* When there is a reception or a luncheon the blessing over the bread—the *Motzi*—also is recited. The bread is called a *challah.*

Obligations of a Jew

These are the obligations of a Jew without measure,

whose reward, too, is without measure:

—*to honor your father and mother,*

—*to perform acts of love and kindness,*

—*to attend the house of study,*

—*to welcome the stranger,*

—*to visit the sick*

—*to rejoice with bride and groom,*

—*to accompany the dead to the grave,*

—*to pray with sincerity,*

—*to make peace when there is strife.*

And the study of Torah is equal to them all,
because it leads to them all.

Talmud, Shabbat 127a

Chapter Six
The Jewish Way of Life

FROM THE TIME JEWS ARE BORN UNTIL WE DIE there are religious ceremonies to be observed. Just as there are differences of opinion among Christians about the observance of their practices, so Jews also interpret their lifecycle events in different ways. However, Orthodox, Conservative and Reform Judaism all agree that the ceremonies which are part of the birth-to-death cycle are important in the life of every Jew.

When the Baby is Born

Mazal Tov—"Congratulations and good luck"—is the happy wish which greets the proud parents of newborn Jewish babies. And with the same breath comes the question, "What is the child's name?"

Jewish children of European descent usually are given names both in English and Hebrew. These names often are taken directly from the names of relatives who have passed away. Many English names are direct translations from the Hebrew. Examples are, David, Samuel, Joseph, Miriam, and Sarah. Sometimes, only the first letter of the relative's Hebrew name is used. Thus the Hebrew *Joash* may become Jerrold or Jeffrey. In Hebrew, however, the child is still called *Joash*.

At other times, Jewish parents will use the meaning of the Hebrew name to choose an English name, regardless of the first letter. Thus, a child named *Yonatan* in Hebrew could very well be called Jeffrey in English, for both names mean "gift of God." Still other parents select an English name of their own choosing, retaining only in Hebrew the relationship with the relatives. The Jewish way of selecting Hebrew and English names is the same for both boys and girls.

Jews of Spanish descent and from the Mediterranian—*Sephardic Jews*—will often name their children in honor of living relatives

Traditionally a child is known as the son or daughter of the father. For example, a boy is called, in Hebrew, *Yonatan ben Yehudah*—"Jonathan, the son of Judah." Likewise, a girl may be called *Shoshanah bat Yehudah*--"Susan, the daughter of Judah." Today it is customary to name children as the son or daughter of both the father and the mother, such as Jonathan, the son of Judah and Miriam, or Susan, the daughter of Judah and Miriam.

The ceremony of naming girls takes place in the synagogue during a worship service. A boy is named at a special ceremony of circumcision—*Brit Milah*—which takes place eight days after his birth.

In Reform temples, the new parents often attend services as soon as the mother is able. The rabbi calls the father and the mother, and, if possible, the newborn infant before the open Ark. There he blesses them and presents the parents with an official naming certificate. In many congregations the newborns also are enrolled in the cradle roll, which registers them as future members of the religious school when they reach pre-school or kindergarten age.

During the Festival of Tabernacles—*Sukkot*—a consecration ceremony is held for boys and girls entering the kindergarten class.

Educating a Jewish Child

The Jewish People hold education in great regard. The *Talmud* (*Mishnah Shabbat* 11.6) teaches that the world endures only for the sake of the breath out of the mouths of children who go to school. The term *Torah*, which ordinarily refers to the scroll in the Holy Ark in the house of worship, has an added meaning——education. The phrase "to learn *Torah*" implies that education is a person's greatest wealth. Likewise, the Hebrew term for education comes from the same root as the Hebrew word for dedication. Jewish life is dedicated to the education of its people.

In Reform temples, Jewish children begin their formal Jewish education with pre-school and enter kindergarten at the age of five. Most religious schools meet on Saturday and/or Sunday mornings. In the religious school children study the Jewish holy days, the history of the Jewish People, and the Bible and literature of Judaism. They become familiar with the prayers of their people, and deal with the problems which are associated with being Jewish. They also study the religions of their neighbors so that they may live better with them. Another important part of a Jewish child's education is the folk and religious music they hear, sing and dance in school and synagogue.

After eleven years of study graduation from the religious school is held. This ceremony is known as Confirmation and is held at Pentecost—*Shavuot*. Just as our ancestors said to Moses at Mount Sinai, "We shall do and we shall listen," so modern

Jewish children also affirm their faith in Judaism by repeating these same words of the Bible. (Exod. 24:7)

However, Confirmation does not mean that the young people are now full members of the synagogue. Confirmation is just one milestone in the continuous road of Jewish education. After Confirmation comes the youth group program. Some congregations also bestow honorary junior memberships on their confirmands.

In addition to the subjects which they learn in English in the religious school, many Jewish boys and girls also study Hebrew. Some religious schools require two additional afternoons of Hebrew study during the week as part of the *Bar* or *Bat Mitzvah* and the Confirmation program. In many instances Hebrew study in the afternoon classes is voluntary.

When Jewish boys and girls are thirteen years of age and have studied Hebrew, they may lead the prayer service and read from the *Torah* at a worship service. By so doing, the boy becomes a "Son of the Commandment" or *Bar Mitzvah*, and the girl becomes a "Daughter of the Commandment" or *Bat Mitzvah*.

In those Orthodox and some Conservative congregations where *Bat Mitzvah* for girls is celebrated, the ceremony takes place at the age of twelve. The *Bar Mitzvah* for boys always occurs at the age of thirteen, unless there are extenuating circumstances. In Reform congregations, both *Bar* and *Bat Mitzvah* are celebrated at the age of thirteen. Confirmation, usually the equivalent of the first two years of Jewish high school education, also is stressed in addition to *Bar* and *Bat Mitzvah*.

Most Jewish children attend public school and, in addition, are enrolled in separate religious school and weekday afternoon classes at their synagogue. However, just as there are private Catholic and Protestant parochial schools, so there is a growing number of Jewish Day Schools and Jewish High Schools where both general and religious subjects are taught.

Choosing a Life Partner

Jewish tradition holds that marriage provides the most desirable way of continuing the human race. The first in the order of the 613 commandments which Judaism counts in the *Torah* is, "Be fruitful and multiply." (Genesis 1:28) The Rabbis interpreted this to mean that the goal for each man should be to have at least two children, one of whom is to be a boy who can carry on the family name. The Hebrew name for marriage is *Kiddushin*, which means "holiness." Judaism holds marriage to be a holy way of life.

Jewish weddings are held either in a synagogue, home, garden setting or a special banquet hall. In most weddings the bride is dressed in white.

Many older traditions have been revived in the last decade. These specific events or rituals are marked with a ✿.

✿ The ceremony may begin with two separate receptions in different rooms. The bride, usually sitting on a large, raised and decorated chair, is attended to by other women. There she greets the wedding guests as they arrive. It is everyone's responsibility to make the bride happy.

✿ At the same time, the groom and male members of the wedding are seated around a table in another room. Songs are sung, the groom is toasted and someone teaches a bit of *Torah*.

At the groom's reception, the wedding contract is reviewed and signed by the official witnesses.

✿ At the proper time, the groom is accompanied by the men to the bride where a short veiling ceremony —*Bedeken*—takes place. The groom places the veil over the bride's face. This ceremony is derived from the Biblical story of Jacob who married the wrong woman because she was hidden behind a veil. With the veiling ceremony, the groom now is sure he has the right bride.

The groom and his best man, together with the rabbi, gather under the *chuppah,* a tent-like structure made of cloth or flowers symbolizing the couples new home. The ushers and maids-of-honor enter. Then comes the bride attended by her parents.

✿ As the bride approaches the groom she circles him three or seven times, depending on the custom of the community. She then stands at the groom's right during the ceremony.

The bride and groom may join hands. The rabbi welcomes them and speaks to them briefly. After asking whether they will take each other as husband and wife—"to love, honor, and cherish all the days of your life,"—the rabbi recites wedding blessings. Following the blessings, a cup of wine is sipped by the bride and groom.

The next part of the ceremony officially unites the couple Jewishly in marriage. The groom places a ring on the finger of his beloved and recites this phrase in Hebrew, "Be consecrated unto me with this ring as my wife according to the laws of Moses and Israel." In many Reform and in some Conservative wedding services, the bride also places a ring on the groom's finger and makes a similar statement.

The ring ceremony is followed by the reading of the Jewish marriage certificate—*Ketubah*—which has been signed by the rabbi and two witnesses. The rabbi and other honored guests then recite the Seven Benedictions—*Sheva Berachot*. At that point the rabbi pronounces the couple to be husband and wife. A glass, covered with cloth, has been placed on the floor. The groom smashes it underfoot and the guests greet them with a hearty *Mazal Tov*, meaning "congratulations and good luck." This tradition is interpreted in many different ways, one of which is to remind us of the destruction of the Temple in ancient Jerusalem.

✡ The new couple then retreats to a room to be alone together for a while. This is called *Yichud*, and is symbolic of the physical consumation of their marriage. In reality, the couple usually has something to eat and a chance to catch their breath before the rounds of picture taking, reception lines, dancing and celebration.

When the couple moves into their home, a small scroll with several passages of Scripture, called a *mezuzah*, is placed upon the doorpost as a sign of consecration. The *mezuzah* symbolizes that this is a Jewish home.

Divorce

Although the goal in every marriage is that a couple become life partners, Jews may divorce. Judaism teaches that sometimes it is better for people to separate and find new mates than to live unhappily with each other. Before seeking a divorce, however, the husband and wife must make serious efforts to solve their problems. Jews are careful about divorce, especially when there are children in the family. Unfortunately, the divorce rate among Jewish couples has risen as a corollary to the growing number of divorces among the general population.

In Jewish tradition, a woman is not permitted to remarry unless she had been given a Jewish divorce document—a *get*—by her husband. Recently, to avoid possible future complications, the Conservative Movement has introduced the practice of requiring the groom to agree in advance of the marriage to give the bride a *get*, should they decide to divorce in the future. Reform Judaism accepts the divorce decree issued by the state to be sufficient and final.

The Jewish Family

The Jewish family—consisting of Jewish parents (a father and a mother), children raised as Jews and linked with Jewish grandparents and Jewish relatives—continues to be the traditional ideal. Many changes, however, are to be found in modern Jewish families. First, the birth rate is very low, and Jews are marrying at an older age and are not reproducing their own numbers. Second, many Jews are marrying non-Jews. Third, due to the increase in divorce, the number of single-parent families is growing. Fourth, the number of gay and lesbian families with (and without) children is increasing.

Orthodox and Conservative Judaism continue to reject homosexuality as an acceptable Jewish life style. Reform and Reconstructionist Judaism, holding fast to the idea of equality, have accepted gay and lesbian Jews in all areas of synagogue life. The Reform and Reconstructionist movements ordain rabbis without regard to their sexual orientation.

Inter-marriage

Marriages involving Jews and non-Jews are not performed in Orthodox and Conservative Judaism unless there is conversion on the part of the non-Jewish person. Reform rabbis are divided about equally on the subject. Some will not participate in such marriages. Those who do officiate generally ask that the couple enroll in a program of Jewish study with or without commitment for conversion on the part of the non-Jewish partner or, minimally, that the couple promise to raise their children as Jews.

In the Jewish tradition, children born of Jewish mothers, are Jewish whether or not the father is Jewish. This principle continues to be followed in Orthodox and Conservative Judaism. Reform Judaism in North America has extended this concept to include children who are born of a Jewish father, who receive a Jewish education, and who are reared as Jews even though the mother may not be Jewish.

Although traditional Jewish life has been organized around the two-parent family, efforts are being made in all branches of Judaism to accommodate the needs of the growing number of single parent families.

When We Die

Jews pray for the recovery of sick people. We ask God to heal them by giving the sick person courage and health. We also pray that God will give wisdom to the doctors and nurses who care for the sick. However, each prayer asks that God's will be done, whatever that may be.

Approaching death, a Jew recites the *Sh'ma*—"Hear, O Israel"—as well as other important verses from the Bible and prayerbook.

Jews hold funeral services. The family and friends gather in a final moment of loving respect. Flowers may be sent in tribute to the departed, unless the family has other wishes. However, modern custom favors a donation to the deceased's favorite charity. Orthodox Jews do not send flowers.

The funeral service consists of prayers and a eulogy in which the rabbi, members of the family, and often friends tell of the praiseworthy aspects of the deceased's life. The Twenty-third Psalm is a favorite scriptural reading.

Most Jews are buried in a wooden casket in a grave. A stone monument or brass marker is placed on the grave about a year later. Sometimes the casket is placed in a mausoleum crypt which has a small marker to identify the person. Cremation is preferred by others. The ashes are placed in an urn and interred either in a grave or a crypt. Some Jews have their ashes scattered.

Orthodox and Conservative Judaism do not favor cremation. They also discourage embalming, except where required by civil law, or when it is necessary to delay burial for the arrival of relatives. In extreme cases the body is kept refrigerated. In every case, the body is attended at all times by a person to ensure that it is treated with the utmost respect. Autopsies are forbidden except under special circumstances.

Both Orthodox and Conservative Judaism encourage the burial of the deceased as soon as possible. Orthodox Judaism places an even greater emphasis upon burial whenever possible without embalming and on the same day in which the death occurs.

The embalming of the body of the deceased has become a more general practice among Reform Jews. Cremation, likewise, is permitted. The burial service usually is held on the second or, if necessary, the third day following the death to allow for arrival of loved ones from long distances.

Judaism teaches that death is as natural as birth. Every person who is born knows that he or she will die, although the individual does not know when death will occur. Judaism accepts the facts of life and death. This does not mean that we are not sad about the loss of our loved ones. We recognize, however, that death is part of life. Therefore, each funeral service concludes with the praise of God—with the *Kaddish* prayer.

Customarily, when the family returns home from the funeral service, they will find a meal prepared for them by friends and neighbors. At evening a *Minyan* service is conducted in the home, and a seven-day candle is lit. A black ribbon, cut as a symbol of mourning, is worn by close family members, a symbol of the ancient Jewish tradition of rending one's garments when in grief.

Seven days of intense mourning, known as "sitting *Shiva*," are observed in Orthodox and Conservative Judaism and three days in Reform Judaism.

During the first eleven months following the death, *Kaddish*, is recited daily by the mourners. Each year on the anniversary of the death—the *Yahrzeit*—a twenty-five hour candle is lit in the home. The relatives of the deceased also go to the synagogue where they recite *Kaddish* and praise the name of God.

Orthodox Judaism holds that there is a Garden of Eden—*Gan Eden*—where the good will be rewarded and a realm called *Gehinnom* for the wicked who are to be punished. The judgment will take place when the *Messiah* comes and the dead are resurrected. However, Jews do not believe that Jesus was nor will be the *Messiah*.

Reform Judaism adheres to the idea of immortality. When people die their souls go back to God, and they are remembered for the things which they have done during their lifetime. The actions of their lives become their living memorial in death. The Reform prayerbook says: *"They still live on earth in the acts of goodness they performed and in the hearts of those who treasure their memory."* Reform Jews do not believe in the existence of the *Gan Eden* nor *Gehinnom*. Conservative Jews vary in their beliefs about life after death.

While Orthodox, Conservative and Reform Judaism may differ on the questions of resurrection and the *Messiah,* they all hold that the body returns to the earth and that the soul goes back to God. Also there is agreement that while death is not the end, the exact nature of life after death cannot be explained in detail.

Funeral services take place in Orthodox, Conservative, and Reform Judaism on all days except the Sabbath, the High Holy Days, and at the beginning and end of the Pilgrim Festivals.

Long ago our Rabbis developed a this-worldly rather than an other-worldly philosophy. Our focus is upon living and doing everything possible to make this world a better place in which to live rather than dwelling on the world-to-come beyond the grave.

Becoming a Rabbi

The word *Rabbi* means "my teacher." A Rabbi is an ordained teacher. One studies ten years to become a Rabbi. After completing a four-year college education, students attend a seminary for six more years of study. During this time they learn to read the literature of Judaism in the original Hebrew. They learn Aramaic, because this was the common language of the people when most of the Holy Books were written. It is the language which Jesus spoke.

The student rabbis also study Jewish history, philosophy and theology. They also become familiar with the education of children and young people as well as with many other skills.

The Conservative, Reconstructionist and Reform Movements ordain women as Rabbis. The Orthodox Movement does not.

There are five main seminaries for the training of rabbis in the United States. The seminary for training Reform rabbis is the oldest and is called the Hebrew Union College-Jewish Institute of Religion, with campuses in Cincinnati, New York and Los Angeles. Conservative rabbis are trained at the Jewish Theological Seminary in New York and at the University of Judaism in Los Angeles. The Reform and Conservative movements both have campuses in Jerusalem where non-Israeli rabbinical students spend time in study. The Isaac Elchanan Yeshivah in New York and the Hebrew Theological College in Chicago prepare students for the Orthodox rabbinate. In addition to these two, there are many other *Yeshivot*, or religious academies, where Orthodox rabbis are ordained. The Reconstructionist Seminary is located in Philadelphia.

The ceremony of graduation for Rabbis is called ordination or *Semichah.* This Hebrew term means actually "the laying on of hands." When one is ordained as a Rabbi in the Reform movement, the president places his hands upon the head or shoulders of the candidate and offers a prayer. This ceremony harkens back to the time when Moses placed his hands on Joshua's head and said, "Be strong and of good courage." (Deut. 31:23) "The laying on of hands" is not practiced currently by the Conservative and Orthodox movements.

Though each movement has its own placement commission, rabbis make their own arrangements with a congregation. They continue in that position for as long a period of time as they and the congregations are satisfied with each other. There is neither a bishop nor any form of hierarchy that tells the rabbi where to serve and how long to minister.

Rabbis belong to a rabbinical organization consisting of graduates of the seminary from which they were ordained. Most Rabbis also participate with their Christian colleagues in the ministerial associations of the cities in which they serve.

The Jewish View of Jesus

The Last Supper, which Jesus and his disciples celebrated was probably a Passover meal. According to many Jewish and non-Jewish scholars, Jesus and his disciples, at the Last Supper, ate *matzah* and the *Pascal* lamb and drank wine in remembrance of the *Exodus* from Egypt. Judaism does not hold the Christian belief that Jesus' participation in this ceremony marked the beginning of a new covenant between God and humanity.

We believe that Jesus was a human being born like all other people, and that he was reared by his family as a Jew. Undoubtably Jesus went to the synagogue, heard the *Torah* read and recited the *Sh'ma.*

When Jesus was asked what was the first and greatest commandment, he quoted the words of the Jewish Scripture in Deuteronomy 6:5: *"You shall love the Lord your God with all your heart, and with all your soul, and with all your might."* (This verse is also found in the New Testament in Matthew 22:37) When Jesus said, *"You shall love your neighbor as yourself"* was the second great commandment, he was quoting the *Book of Leviticus* (19:18) in the *Torah*

When Jesus taught, *"Whatever you would that men should do to you, do you even so to them,"* (Matt. 7:12) his words were very similar to those of the famous Jewish sage Hillel, who lived a generation before Jesus. Hillel taught, *"What is hateful to you, do not do unto your neighbor."*

Similarly, the words of the Lord's Prayer, (Matt. 6:9-15) *"Our Father who art in heaven, hallowed be Thy name. Thy kingdom come...,"* closely resembles the ancient wording of the *Kaddish* prayer: *"Hallowed and sanctified is your great name ... May You speedily establish your kingdom of righteousness on earth."*

We believe that Jesus was a teacher and interpreted Judaism as he understood it—serving people and offering his personal help. He went to those whose needs were not being met either in the Temple of the *Sadducean* priests or in the synagogues of the *Pharisaic* rabbis. Jesus, in performing this most helpful service, became neither a non-Jew nor the founder of a new religion. Nor was he a prophet or a rabbi. He was never ordained.

The Messiah

As Jews, we do not accept the idea that Jesus is, or was, the *Messiah* or the only way of salvation. The Jewish definition of *Messiah* is that of a <u>human</u>, military/political leader who will free the Jewish People from oppression by others, and who will then create a Jewish state and social order respected by all other nations. The Christian definition of *Messiah* is different.

Christians believe that the *Messiah* is a <u>divine being</u> who came to earth in the form of a human being and that his second coming will signal the end of days. It is most important when reading or discussing the idea of *Messiah* that each member of the discussion understand which definition is being used.

Conclusions

In Judaism there is no dogma, no fixed creed with which a Jewish person must agree completely. The test of loyalty in Judaism is how we act and not how we think. Our Rabbis taught: "The righteous of all people have a share in the world to come." (*Tosefta Sanhedrin* 13.2)

Our Rabbis have explained very clearly that being Jewish does not guarantee our being rewarded either in this life or in life after death. According to them, the test for all people, Jewish and non-Jewish alike, is not what we believe but how we live with ourselves and with other people. They held that righteousness and lovingkindness (justice and compassion) are the primary requirements for everybody, and that those who wish to become Jewish can do so by voluntarily taking on the extra teachings and practices of Judaism.

All interpretations of Judaism hold that salvation can be found through many faiths, if those religions teach their followers to live together with people of all religions in righteousness and lovingkindness.

Each year many non-Jews in the United States convert to Judaism. The are called *Jews by Choice* because they have chosen to do so. After a period of study they go through a brief ceremony in which they promise to pattern their lives on the teachings of Judaism. Although Reform Judaism has developed an outreach program for bringing unaffiliated non-Jews into Judaism and especially those non-Jews who are married to Jewish partners, we do not, as a rule, send out missionaries to convert others to our faith. Recently, some Conservative rabbis also have begun to develop an outreach program.

However, all who wish to convert to Judaism are welcome to do so upon the completion of a program of study and the commitment to live a Jewish life, to raise their children as Jews, and to identify with the Jewish People.

✡

Publisher's Suggested Basic Reading List

If you are just getting started on your journey to a better understanding of Judaism, or if you wish to increase your current knowledge, the publisher suggests the following list of books, taken from a recent national survey. All are very readable and will lead to a desire to want to know more about each subject. Most are available in or through local bookstores. Most are also available in trade paperback.

Jews are known to be one of the largest reading groups in America. Most Jewish homes are easily identified by the large number of books on shelves and tables. Being the *People of the Book* has taken on a new connotation based on the high level of book buying and book reading by the average Jewish family.

Religion

To Life: A Celebration of Jewish Being and Thinking, by Harold Kushner, Little Brown & Co. This is one of the most beautiful explanations of modern Judaism, and it is written from the heart by the author of *When Bad Things Happen to Good People.* (Available in paperback.)

Jewish Literacy, The Most Important Things to Know About the Jewish Religion, Its People, and Its History, by Rabbi Joseph Telushkin, William Morrow and Co. This is probably the most important reference book on Judaism written to date. Each Jewish concept and idea is discussed in a one-page summary by an author who writes for the average person.

The Nine Questions People Ask About Judaism, by Rabbi Joseph Telushkin and Dennis Prager. This is a book about Judaism that is written in very rational down-to-earth terms. (Available in paperback.)

Basic Judaism, by Milton Steinberg. This is the classic starting book on Judaism written this century. (Available in paperback.)

This Is My God, by Herman Wouk. This is a very personal account of a traditional Jew, who also is popular writer of modern novels, such as *The Winds of War* and *War and Remembrance.* (Available in paperback.)

Historical

Jews, God and History, by Max Dimont. This book is everyone's guide to the history of the Jewish people. Written by a journalist and not an historian, this is probably one of the most-read Jewish books of this century. (Available in paperback.)

A Sacred Trust: Stories of Jewish Heritage and History (Three Volumes), by Rabbi Eugene and Annette Labovitz, Isaac Nathan Publishing Co. Two thousand years of Jewish history are covered, from the fall of the Second Temple in Jerusalem in 70 C.E. until, and including, the founding of the State of Israel, told in the traditional Jewish story format. (Available in paperback directly from this publisher.)

Novels

The Source, by James A. Michener. This novel follows the history of the Holy Land and its people from the earliest time of pre-history until modern times. (Available in paperback.)

Exodus, by Leon Uris. This is a novel about the redemption of the survivors of the Holocaust of World War II and the founding of the modern State of Israel. (Available in paperback.)

Scriptures

The Tanakh, Jewish Publication Society. This is one of the most recent and best accepted translations of the Hebrew Scriptures from the traditional Hebrew text. (Now available on CD.)

The Torah: A Modern Commentary, by Gunther Plaut and Bernard Bamberger, UAHC Press. This translation of the Hebrew Scriptures includes detailed commentaries on almost every aspect of the original writings. It includes a modern translation, the actual Hebrew text and commentaries, as well as detailed essays. It also contains the weekly and special Haftorah selections in English and Hebrew. A new commentary of the *Haftarahs* has recently been completed by Rabbi Plaut and published by the UAHC Press.

Pronunciation of Hebrew Words

There are two pronunciations of Hebrew in use today. The Sephardic dialect (*Sepharad* means "Spain" in Hebrew) is used in Israel and among many groups in the United States.

The Ashkenazic dialect (*Ashkenaz* means "Germany" in Hebrew) is the form which was brought to the United States by the large central and eastern European migration. However, there is a trend among many congregations to use the Sephardic dialect, a form regarded by many to be the scientifically more accurate way of pronouncing Hebrew.

Both Sephardic and Ashkenazic Hebrew use the identical alphabet. The primary difference rests in the manner of pronunciation of several consonants and vowels.

It will be helpful to keep in mind that, wherever the letters "ch" are written together, they are pronounced almost like a German guttural "Ch". For example, there is no sound in Hebrew like the "ch" in "church." This rule holds for Sephardic and Ashkenazic Hebrew alike.

The first column of the Glossary lists many of the Hebrew terms used in this book. The second column gives the pronunciation according to the Sephardic pronunciation. The terms listed in the third column are the Ashkenazic equivalents.

Ten *Yiddish* terms are included in this manuscript. *Yiddish* is a language which many Jewish people use, particularly those whose origins were in Eastern Europe. It is based on the German of the sixteenth century but uses the letters of the Hebrew alphabet. These words are: *dreidel, gantz, Gut Shabbos, halb, hamantaschen, latkes, nisht, schul, shtel,* and *Yahrzeit.*

Terms	Pronunciation	
	Sephardic	**Ashkenazic**
Adonai	Ah-doh-nai	Ah-doh-noi
Afikomen	Ah-fee-koh-mehn	Ah-fee-koh-mehn
Aron	Ah-rohn	Ah-rohn
Hakodesh	Hah-koh-desh	Hah-koh-desh
Bar Mitzvah	Bahr Mitz-vah	Bahr Mitz-vaw
Bimah	Bihm-mah	Bihm-maw
Challah	Chahl-lah	Chahl-law
Chanukah	Chah-noo-kah	Chah-noo-kaw
Charoset	Chah-roh-seht	Chah-roh-sehs
Chazzan	Chahz-zahn	Chahz-zawn
Chupah	Choop-pah	Choop-paw
Echad	Eh-Chahd	Eh-chawd
Elohenu	Eh-loh-hay-noo	Eh-loh-hay-noo
Etrog	Eht-rohg	Ehs-rohg
Gehinnom	Gay-hin-nohm	Gay-hin-nohm
Haftarah	Hahf-tah-rah	Hahf-taw-raw
Haggadah	Hahg-gah-dah	Hahg-gaw-daw
Havdalah	Hahv-dah-lah	Hahv-daw-law
Kaddish	Kahd-deesh	Kahd-deesh
Kiddush	Kid-doosh	Kid-doosh
Kol Nidre	Kawl-Nid-ray	Kawl-Nid-ray
Lag B'Omer	Lahg-B-Oh-mehr	Lahg-B-Oh-mehr
Lulav	Loo-lahv	Loo-Lawv
Machzor	Mahch-zohr	Mahch-zohr
Matzah	Mah-tzah	Mah-tzaw
Mazal Tov	Mah-zahl Tohv	Mah-zawl Tohv
Megillah	M-gil-lah	M-gil-law
Menorah	M-nor-rah	M-noh-raw
Mezuzah	M-zoo-zah	M-zoo-zaw
Minyan	Min-yahn	Min-yawn
Motzi	Moh-tzee	Moh-tzee
Ner Tamid	Nayr Tah-meed	Nayr Taw-meed
Neshamah	N-Shah-mah-	N-Shaw-maw-
Yeterah	Y-tay-rah	Y-say-raw
Pesach	Peh-sahch	Peh-sahch
Purim	Poo-reem	Poo-reem
Rosh	Rohsh	Rohsh
Hashanah	Hah-shah-nah	Hah-shaw-naw
Seder	Say-dehr	Say-dehr
Semichah	S-mee-chah	S-mee-chaw
Shabbat	Shahb-baht	Shab-baws
Shalom	Shah-lohm	Shaw-lohm
Shammash	Shahm-mahsh	Shahm-mawsh
Shavuot	Shah-voo-oht	Shah-voo-ohs
Sh'ma	Sh-mah	Sh-mah
Shofar	Shoh-fahr	Shoh-fawr
Siddur	Sid-door	Sid-door
Sofer	Soh-fayr	Soh-fayr
Sukkah	Sook-kah	Sook-kaw
Sukkot	Sook-koht	Sook-kohs
Tallit	Tahl-leet	Tahl-lees
Tefillin	T-fil-leen	T-fil-leen
Tishah B'Av	Tsih-ah B-ahv	Tish-aw B-awv
Torah	Toh-rah	Toh-raw
Tu B-shvaht	Too B-shvaht	Too B-shvaht
Yisrael	Yis-rah-ayl	Yis-raw-ayl
Yom Kippur	Yohm Kip-poor	Yohm Kip-poor

Author's Note

When I was a congregational Rabbi, I was flooded with requests from both Protestant and Catholic churches to visit our Temple. To make it easier on myself and the congregation, invitations were extended for a one-day gathering. Over 2,000 non-Jews flocked to the Temple. Because of this outpouring, there was an immediate need to train docents to assist in the project. From these training sessions emerged the original version of the present book, called *Our Jewish Neighbors* which was published by Abington Press, a Methodist publisher, at the suggestion of the Executive Director of the local office of the National Conference of Christians and Jews.

At the same time, while serving as the Jewish consultant to a series of 45 Catholic textbooks called *To Live Is Christ*, I was asked to adapt my first book specifically for Catholic School teachers. Soon afterwards *What Catholics Should Know About Jews* was published by W.C. Brown Co.

More than 35 years have passed since *Our Jewish Neighbors* was published. During that time many changes have taken place in the world, including the world of Judaism. The feminist emphasis upon egalitarian relationships between men and women has left a deep imprint. The use of non-sexist language and different ways of thinking about prayer and God have left their mark. The growing desire for more ritual, especially in the wedding ceremony, has become increasingly evident. New ceremonies have emerged around the rites of passage in the life cycle of Jews.

✡

Index